ScottForesman

*Book*Festival

Program Authors

Andrea Butler
Regis University, Denver

Violet Harris
Associate Professor
University of Illinois, Urbana-Champaign

Sam Leaton Sebesta
Professor of Education
University of Washington, Seattle

D1370863

ScottForesman

A Division of HarperCollins*Publishers*

If we can be of any assistance, please call us toll-free: 1-800-554-4411

ISBN: 0-673-81624-9

*Book*Festival celebrates independent reading!

When you put *BookFestival* in your class, kids will discover that magical feeling of choosing a good book, curling up, and reading. That's because *BookFestival* is a supplementary reading program with an extraordinary collection of children's literature. There are funny books, informational books, mystery books, books that make kids fall in love with reading. All of them fit neatly in their own classroom Library Center for easy access and storage. You'll also find exciting literature-based materials to help students take charge of their reading and achieve success independently.

The Best Children's Books

make reading a treat! Kids can choose from the latest storybooks, exciting classics, and popular favorites.

The Library Center

keeps all the books and materials neat and within easy reach. Clear vinyl student portfolios are included.

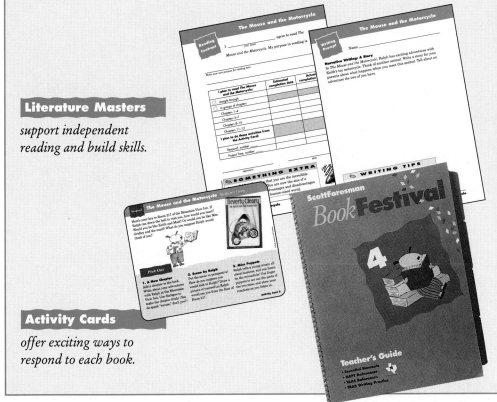

Literature Masters

support independent reading and build skills.

Activity Cards

offer exciting ways to respond to each book.

Writing Masters

help kids practice for the TAAS test.

Teacher's Guide

has quick tips, ideas, and suggestions.

Teacher's Resource Library

provides activities and minimizes planning time.

Teacher's Read-Aloud Library

offers a collection of wonderful stories to share.

Kids practice skills and strategies as they work independently.

You've taught strategies and skills with your literature-based reading program. Now, here's the perfect opportunity to have students practice and apply those skills. *BookFestival* provides materials that extend and reinforce important reading strategies and skills as kids work independently. Whether it's building background before reading, aiding comprehension with graphic organizers, or working in literature circles, each book comes with its own mind-stretching activities that make students responsible for their reading. Of course, it just wouldn't be a festival if these activities weren't fun, active, and engaging.

Activity Cards extend the reading.

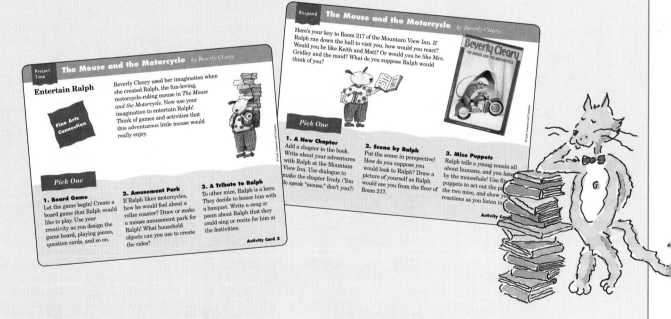

Response Activities

invite kids to respond to the literature through writing, drawing, dramatizing, and speaking.

Cross-curricular Projects

connect reading and writing with other school subjects, such as science, social studies, or math.

Literature Masters build strategic readers.

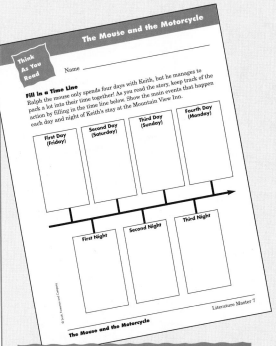

Reading Contracts

show students how to plan their reading and set purposes.

Prior Knowledge Masters

promote language and concept development.

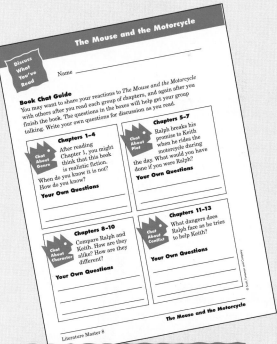

Graphic Organizers

aid understanding and reinforce comprehension skills.

Literature Circle Guides

invite thoughtful responses to the reading and help students work in small groups.

The Teacher's Guide is a simple, quick, and clear idea book.

Since *BookFestival* is designed for independent reading, we kept the Teacher's Guide clean and uncluttered. There are no lengthy directions, no overload of details, no unnecessary facts. What you will find is concise information to support kids' independent reading as they practice and apply strategies and skills. Planning tips and book-by-book notes, as well as clear references to the Texas Essential Elements, TAAS, and NAPT objectives, make it easy to track students' success. Naturally, you'll want to use only the information you need. Scan the pages for good ideas. It's simple and it's quick.

Highlights

of each book provide simple, at-a-glance notes on students, resources, themes, books, and authors.

Teaching Options

help you meet individual needs, address multicultural topics, and build vocabulary strategies.

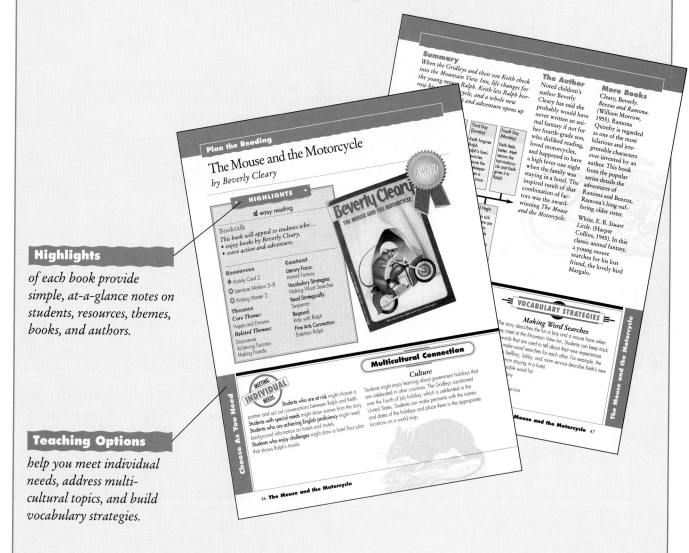

Notes on Literature Masters and Activity Cards

make it easy to keep tabs on students. Texas Essential Elements, TAAS objectives, and NAPT objectives are clearly identified.

Before Reading

⭐ Literature Master 5
Use Prereading Strategies
Help students fill out the Reading Contract for *The Mouse and the Motorcycle*. Suggest that students preview the table of contents, the book cover, and the illustrations. They might also read Activity Card 2 to choose activities for after reading. Encourage students to amend their contracts as needed.
(preview; set purpose)

⭐ Literature Master 6
Build Language and Concepts
Students can use their creativity and their knowledge about mice to solve the problems on Literature Master 6. Have students return to this page and note how Ralph solved some of these problems as they read the story. ✏️
(activate prior knowledge)

During Reading

⑦ Literature Master 7
Read Strategically
A lot of action is packed into the four days and three nights written about in *The Mouse and the Motorcycle*. Students might use this time line to keep track of the events in the story. ✏️
(comprehension skill: sequence)

⑧ Literature Master 8
Share and Discuss
The Book Chat Guide can be used by students to jot down their questions and comments. Encourage students to use these notes as they discuss Ralph's adventures during their book chat. 💬👥
(speaking and listening)

EEk2 Comprehension Strategies (Bi) Set an appropriate purpose for reading and/or listening
NAPT Reading Comprehension Draw conclusions and make inferences

EEk2 Comprehension Strategies (Bii) Develop literal meaning through recognition of details and sequential order
TAAS Reading Comprehension Identify supporting ideas in a variety of written texts (sequence)

Assess / Wrap Up

◼ CHECK ON THE READING ◼

Conference with students after they finish reading *The Mouse and the Motorcycle*. Suggest that they use their time lines to remind them of events in the story. These questions might help you assess students' understanding of the story:

• Why do Keith and Ralph get along? *(Can students describe the interests and personality traits that both characters share?)*

• How does Ralph solve problems? *(Do students appreciate Ralph's creativity and willingness to take risks? Can they cite specific examples?)*

• How might Ralph's life change after the gift of the motorcycle? *(Are students able to verbalize what they think might happen in the future?)*

(See also Assessment Check in the BookFestival assessment component.)

48 **The Mouse and the Motorcycle**

After Reading

② Activity Card 2
Respond (Side 1)
Students check into the Mountain View Inn and create an adventure of their own with Ralph the mouse. Remind students to use details from the book but to also use their imaginations to include themselves in the action.
(critical and creative thinking)

The Activity Card suggests these ideas:
1. **A New Chapter** Students write a chapter about their adventures with Ralph. ✏️
(narrative writing)
2. **Scene by Ralph** Students draw themselves from Ralph's perspective.
(visualize)
3. **Mice Puppets** Students create a dialogue and perform it with finger puppets. 💬
(dramatize)

② Activity Card 2
Fine Arts Connection (Side 2)
Students can use their knowledge of Ralph the mouse and their creativity to think of ways to entertain him.
(respond critically and creatively)

The Activity Card suggests these ideas:
1. **Board Game** Students create a board game for Ralph to play.
(respond creatively)
2. **Amusement Park** Students draw or make a mouse amusement park using household objects.
(visualize)
3. **A Tribute to Ralph** Students write a poem or song honoring Ralph.
(expressive writing)

EEc1 Speaking (Biii) Entertain others with stories, poems, and dramatic activities
EEk2 Literary Appreciation (Diii) Use setting, characterization, story line, author's technique, and point of view to gain meaning

EEc1 Fine Arts (Bii) Express individual ideas, thoughts, and feelings in simple media including drawing, painting, printmaking, construction and modeling three-dimensional forms
EEk2 Literary Appreciation (Dv) Participate in cooperative learning and a variety of oral activities to elicit meaning from written text

---

ASSESS STUDENTS' ACTIVITIES

...nd: Do students
...heir creativity in
...ng part of this
... fantasy?

• **Fine Arts Connection:** Do students' projects show their inventiveness? Do they understand what would appeal to Ralph?

WRAP UP

• **Connect Home and School:** Invite students to compile a list of books by Beverly Cleary and survey their family members about which ones they have read. Which books are most popular? Students can report their findings to the class.

The Mouse and the Motorcycle 49

Assessment and Home-school Options

help you check students' comprehension and provide home-school connections.

Look for These Learning Opportunities!

╫╫╫ Group

╫╫ Partner

💬 Speaking

👤 Listening

📁 Assessment Portfolio Possibility

✏️ Writing Opportunity

⭐ Literature Master

◆ Activity Card

Texas writing practice leads to success on the TAAS test.

We want to help you give your students every advantage. That's why we designed special Texas Writing Masters that familiarize kids with the TAAS writing test. Students learn the test format by responding to the same types of writing prompts they'll encounter on the TAAS test. They get specific tips on how to respond directly and clearly to the writing prompts. There's even a model for each different writing mode. All of which will help your students pass the test with flying colors!

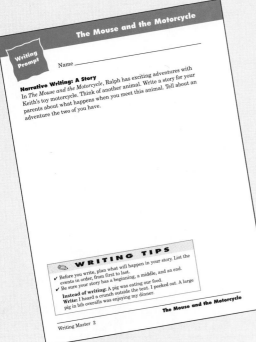

The Mouse and the Motorcycle

Writing Prompt

Name _____

Narrative Writing: A Story
In *The Mouse and the Motorcycle*, Ralph has exciting adventures with Keith's toy motorcycle. Think of another animal. Write a story for your parents about what happens when you meet this animal. Tell about an adventure the two of you have.

🖉 **WRITING TIPS**

✔ Before you write, plan what will happen in your story. List the events in order, from first to last.
✔ Be sure your story has a beginning, a middle, and an end.
Instead of writing: A pig was eating our food.
Write: I heard a crunch outside the tent. I peeked out. A large pig in bib overalls was enjoying my dinner.

Writing Master 2   **The Mouse and the Motorcycle**

Night Markets

Writing Model

Name _____

Explanatory Writing: A Letter
Night Markets describes the way people mix, shape, and bake 1,200 dozen rolls for restaurants and stores each night of the week. Write a letter to your friend telling how to make a dish you enjoy eating. Tell what you do first. Then tell about the other steps to take in making the dish.

Dear Darcy,

    Fruit juice Popsicles taste great, and they're easy to make. You'll need three things: an empty ice cube tray, a bunch of toothpicks, and fruit juice.
    Here's how to make the Popsicles. First, set a toothpick in each cup of the tray. Next, pour fruit juice into each cup. Then stick the tray into the freezer and wait. Don't take the tray out too soon, or you might spoil the Popsicles. Once the juice is frozen, pull out a Popsicle by grabbing the toothpick. I hope you like them!

       Your Friend,
        Kate

🖉 **WRITING TIPS**

✔ List the steps you'd take to make the dish in the order that you would do them.
✔ When you write, describe each step separately.
✔ Use words such as *first, next,* and *last* to show where one step ends and the next one begins.
✔ Tell your readers everything they'll need to know.
Instead of writing: Heat the milk, but first peel the apples.
Write: First peel the apples. Then heat the milk for two minutes.

Writing Master 18   **Night Markets**

Writing Prompts

help students prepare for the TAAS test by using the same types of writing prompts. Built-in writing tips are included.

Writing Models

let kids see how they can structure and organize their writing. There's one model for each writing type on the TAAS test.

TAAS Writing Practice

Writing Masters and Writing Prompts link TAAS Writing Practice to *BookFestival* literature.

Writing Master	TAAS Writing Prompt	Selection
1	Descriptive Writing: A Letter (Informative/Descriptive)	*The Girl Who Loved the Wind*
2	Narrative Writing: A Story (Expressive/Narrative)	*The Mouse and the Motorcycle*
3	Descriptive Writing: A Character Sketch (Informative/Descriptive)	*There's a Boy in the Girls' Bathroom*
4	Explanatory Writing: A Letter (Informative/Narrative)	*Night Markets*
5	Narrative Writing: A Story (Expressive/Narrative)	*Sidewalk Story*
6	Informative Writing: An Article (Informative/Classificatory)	*Tales of a Fourth Grade Nothing*
7	Persuasive Writing: A Letter (Persuasive/Descriptive)	*Staying Nine*
8	Explanatory Writing: An Article (Informative/Narrative)	*Willie Mays, Young Superstar*
9	Informative Writing: A Composition (Informative/Classificatory)	*Esio Trot*
10	Informative Writing: A Letter (Informative/Classificatory)	*Sarah, Plain and Tall*
11	Persuasive Writing: A Letter (Persuasive/Descriptive)	*Grandma Moses, Painter of Rural America*
12	Descriptive Writing: A Composition (Informative/Descriptive)	*Kickle Snifters and Other Fearsome Creatures*
13	Explanatory Writing: A Report (Informative/Narrative)	*The Case of the Sabotaged School Play*
14	Persuasive Writing: A Composition (Persuasive/Descriptive)	*From Anna*
15	Narrative Writing: A Story (Expressive/Narrative)	*The Adventures of Spider*

☐ Writing models are keyed to lessons 1, 2, 4, 6, and 7.

Book Festival Authors

Andrea Butler

Andrea Butler taught grades K-6 in Australian schools for many years before becoming a National Language Consultant in Australia. Along with co-author Jan Turbill, Andrea has written many resource books, including *The Story Box in the Classroom* and *Towards a Reading/Writing Classroom*. For ScottForesman, Andrea served as an author of *Celebrate Reading!* and is the featured author of the videotape *Celebrating the Literature-Based Classroom*. She has been the guiding force in integrating the techniques of supported reading into the *Celebrate Reading!* program.

Violet J. Harris

Violet Harris is Associate Professor at the University of Illinois at Champaign-Urbana, where she teaches courses in children's literature. She is also a Senior Scientist with the Center for the Study of Reading. Dr. Harris received her B.A. in history from Oberlin College in Ohio, an M.A. in Reading from Atlanta University, and a Ph.D. in Reading Education from the University of Georgia. Dr. Harris is very active in both the National Reading Conference and the National Council of Teachers of English. She received the Spencer Foundation Scholarship for 1990-1991 from the National Academy of Education and is a *Celebrate Reading!* author.

Sam Leaton Sebesta

Dr. Sebesta is a Professor in the College of Education at the University of Washington in Seattle. Before coming to the University in 1963, Dr. Sebesta taught at the elementary school level, grades 1-8. He has conducted many workshops and speeches throughout the United States, Europe, Canada, and Australia, and is the author of *Literature for Thursday's Child* (with William J. Iverson) and other books, articles, and assorted publications. In 1986, Dr. Sebesta received the Arbuthnot Award for "Outstanding Teacher of Children's Literature," and in 1988, the "Education in Literacy Award." Dr. Sebesta is an author of ScottForesman's *Celebrate Reading!* program.

Texas Consultants

Jackie Harland
Lubbock Independent
School District

Laura Espensen
North East Independent
School District

Sherri Wakeland
Coppell Independent
School District

Eva G. Gonzalez
Ysleta Independent
School District

Jerry Leinart
Lone Oak Independent
School District

Judy Bratton
Grape Creek–Pulliam
Independent School
District

Linda Lively
Pasadena Independent
School District

Maridell F. Fryar
Midland Independent
School District

Managing *BookFestival*

Getting Started

How do I use *BookFestival* in my classroom? How you use *BookFestival* to enhance your current reading program will depend not only on the needs, interests, and attention span of your students, but also on you—on the way you teach and the way you manage your classroom. Since *BookFestival* enables students to be self-directed, it is easy to manage, providing you with greater flexibility.

Managing the Classroom

A good way to foster and nourish students' independence is to set up the books and materials so that students know when and where they can either read independently or find and complete Literature Masters or response activities.

The Library Center
enables students to self-select trade books.

Activity Cards
can be stored in the Library Center for easy access.

Literature Masters
can be placed near the Library Center for independent skills practice.

Writing Masters
can be made available for independent writing activities at the Library Center or at a writing center.

Managing the Students

- **Portfolios** are ideal for storing the books and materials that students are using.
- **Book Chat Sign-Up** sheets can be displayed so that students can manage their own discussions about the literature.
- **Contracts** provide you with a way to monitor students' reading progress and work on the response activities.
- **Literature and Writing Masters** can be assigned to individuals as needed.

Matching Students with Books

- *BookFestival* **titles** can be used in any order. Choose a book that supplements your reading program by theme, genre, author or illustrator, content area, or interest. (See pages 14–15 for additional ideas.)
- **A variety of reading levels**—easy, average, and challenging—and high-interest fiction and nonfiction titles make it easy for you to assign reading. (See the Highlights section of Book-by-Book Notes for help in assigning reading.)
- **Highlights and Summary** sections of the Book-by-Book Notes help you introduce a title to students who are selecting books on their own.
- **Rich, appealing literature** covering a wide range of topics makes it easy for students to choose books that interest them.

Matching Students with Each Other

- **Independent readers** will enjoy choosing books from the Library Center.
- **Flexible groups** offer additional ways for students to manage their reading independent of direct teacher guidance.
- **Collaborative, Partner, and Supported Reading** are options for a more interactive reading environment. As you assign reading, pair a fluent reader with a less fluent reader, or group several students who enjoy the same type of literature. Ask a more proficient reader to guide another reader using Supported Reading.

Curriculum Connections

How can *BookFestival* supplement my reading program? *BookFestival* is designed to fit easily into any classroom as an extension of your reading program or as a resource library for independent reading activities. Use the theme-rich literature and cross-curricular Project Time activities to organize your reading program or your entire curriculum around *BookFestival*.

Organizing Your Curriculum Around *BookFestival*

The rich, authentic fiction and nonfiction in *BookFestival* let you naturally connect your curriculum goals and objectives to the books. This example shows how one teacher listed her ideas for cross-curricular connections with one of the books.

Social Studies
- discuss needs and wants
- discuss family relations
- talk about traveling to far-away places

Science
- research weather patterns
- discuss types and directions of winds
- investigate the pros and cons of wind

The Girl Who Loved the Wind

Language Arts
- speaking—tell a folk tale; interview the characters; tell about a new adventure
- writing—explain Danina's feelings in a letter or in a diary entry

Fine Arts
- invent an instrument that sounds like the wind
- write and perform a song about the folk tale
- make paper windmills
- illustrate a story extension

Organizing Themes Around *BookFestival*

Title	Core Theme	Related Themes	Activity Card Cross-Curricular Connection	
The Girl Who Loved the Wind	Hopes and Dreams	Fantasy Wishes Come True Imagination	Fine Arts:	Make a Scroll Write a Ballad Perform a Skit
The Mouse and the Motorcycle	Hopes and Dreams	Discoveries Achieving Success Making Friends	Fine Arts:	Board Game Amusement Park A Tribute to Ralph
There's a Boy in the Girls' Bathroom	School Stories	Dreamers and Achievers Friendship	Social Studies:	Interviews Cartoons School Facts
Night Markets	Learning Outside of School	Transportation Food Learning about the World	Social Studies:	Draw a Map Make a List Write an Article
Sidewalk Story	Caring	Friends and Families Wishes Come True Making It Happen	Math:	Do Lunch Spend a Million Figure It Out
Tales of a Fourth Grade Nothing	Caring	Family Life Wishes Come True Pet Stories	Fine Arts:	Cartoon Story Letters to Peter Cover Illustration
Staying Nine	Family Customs	Celebrations Growing Up Friends and Family	Science:	Definitions Personal Reactions Illustrations
Willie Mays: Young Superstar	Family Support	Dreamers and Achievers Let's Find Out	Language Arts:	Interviews Contributions Portraits
Esio Trot	Animals Matter	Pet Stories Problem Solving Wishes Come True	Math:	Popular Pets Pet Report Feeding Your Pet
Sarah, Plain and Tall	Places of the Past	Pioneers Life on a Farm All Kinds of Families	Social Studies:	Current Events Recipes or Instructions Advertisements
Grandma Moses: Painter of Rural America	Ways of Seeing	Nature Imagination Times Past	Social Studies:	Everyday Scenes Interview Time Skit from the Future
Kickle Snifters and Other Fearsome Critters	Creativity	Imagination Tall Tales Animal Stories	Language Arts:	Models Illustrated Catalog Zoo Map
The Case of the Sabotaged School Play	Being a Close Observer	Mysteries Discoveries Investigations	Fine Arts:	Write It Down Get Set Costume Design
From Anna	Standing Up for Your Beliefs	Families Immigrants Overcoming Challenges	Science:	Draw a Diagram Do Some Research Find Optical Illusions
The Adventures of Spider	Courage in Folk Tales	Animal Tales Storytelling Having Fun	Language Arts:	Write Your Story Plan a Puppet Show Share a Story

Skills Practice

How does *BookFestival* help students practice reading strategies and skills? *BookFestival's* student materials—books, Literature Masters, Writing Masters, and Activity Cards—enable students to apply reading skills and strategies. The teacher's Book-by-Book Notes explain what skills are being covered and even suggest optional activities for the whole class or small groups of students.

Supporting Students

Book-by-Book Notes in the Teacher's Guide provide information to help you assist students in selecting and using appropriate reading strategies as they work independently on Literature Masters. These notes also include optional mini-lessons highlighting vocabulary and literary elements.

Teacher's Guide
provides optional activities for helping students focus on skills and strategies.

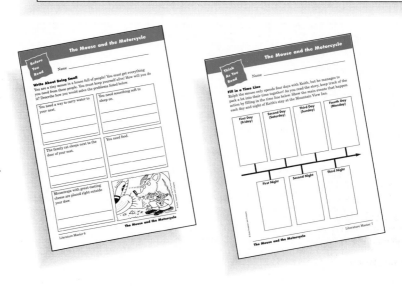

LITERARY FOCUS

Animal Fantasy

Remind students that a fantasy is a story that could not really happen. An animal fantasy is a story in which animals act like people.

Activity: As students read *The Mouse and the Motorcycle*, they can list the ways that Ralph acts like a person and how he acts like a mouse. Then have students explain why most people would not like to share a hotel room with a mouse.

VOCABULARY STRATEGIES

Making Word Searches

The story describes the fun a boy and a mouse have when they meet at the Mountain View Inn. Students can keep track of words that are used to tell about their new experiences and make word searches for each other. For example, the words *bellboy, lobby,* and *room service* describe Keith's new experience staying in a hotel.

A possible word list:
- bellboy
- lobby
- room service

The Mouse and the Motorcycle 47

Literature Masters
guide students as they practice prereading strategies, activate prior knowledge, and read strategically.

Skills and Strategies Overview

Title	Comprehension Skill	Literary Focus
The Girl Who Loved the Wind	Summarize	Setting
The Mouse and the Motorcycle	Sequence	Animal fantasy
There's a Boy in the Girls' Bathroom	Details and facts	Realistic fiction
Night Markets	Main idea; details and facts	Photo essay
Sidewalk Story	Draw conclusions	Theme
Tales of a Fourth Grade Nothing	Cause and effect	Characterization
Staying Nine	Sequence	Point of view
Willie Mays: Young Superstar	Sequence	Narrative nonfiction
Esio Trot	Summarize	Dialogue
Sarah, Plain and Tall	Compare and contrast	Historical fiction
Grandma Moses: Painter of Rural America	Details and facts	Biography
Kickle Snifters and Other Fearsome Critters	Classify	Figurative language
The Case of the Sabotaged School Play	Cause and effect	Plot
From Anna	Draw conclusions	Mood
The Adventures of Spider	Compare and contrast	Folk tales

Meeting Individual Needs

How can I use literature to provide all students equal access to reading and writing? *BookFestival* is an excellent resource for meeting individual needs since authentic literature helps all students to increase their ability to read and write. Book-by-Book Notes suggest teaching options that include multisensory and tactile strategies for helping your students throughout the reading process. Reading Contracts allow you to pace reading and instruction to meet the needs of each student.

At Risk Students

Students who are at risk may also benefit from
- creating predictable text through discussion and shared writing.
- hearing stories read aloud.
- doing oral rereadings and paired readings.
- hands-on literature-response activities.
- having meanings explained together with concrete objects.
- being reminded to use illustrations and photos in books to help clarify the text.
- mini-lessons about key concepts.
- spending more time talking about concepts before they read.

Special Needs Students

Students with special needs may also benefit from
- working in a variety of modalities.
- tape recording oral readings.
- dramatizing scenes from a book.
- planning puppet plays, designing characters' costumes, creating drawings of settings, and painting characters from memory.
- selecting music to fit the mood and action of a story.
- reading in different settings.
- spending more time one-on-one with a reading partner.
- having more opportunities to predict before reading.

Choose As You Need

MEETING INDIVIDUAL NEEDS

Students who are at risk might choose a partner and act out conversations between Ralph and Keith.

Students with special needs might draw scenes from the story.

Students who are achieving English proficiency might need background information on hotels and motels.

Students who enjoy challenges might draw a hotel floor plan that shows Ralph's travels.

Teacher's Guide
gives suggestions for helping students with reading.

LEP and ESL Students

Students who are achieving English proficiency or who speak nonstandard English may also benefit from

- a print-rich environment.
- modeling of new concepts and of new labels for old concepts.
- hearing stories read aloud.
- having vocabulary and idiomatic expressions explained in context.
- having meaning expressed through personalization, demonstration, dramatization, exemplification, illustration, or definition.
- sharing prior knowledge about other countries.
- spending more time with concrete objects or manipulatives to help them make links to the books.

(For more detailed ideas on using *BookFestival* with second language learners, see pp. 20–21.)

Gifted and Talented Students

Students who enjoy challenges may also benefit from

- comparisons of stories, authors, illustrators, and genres and meaningful activities such as investigations and research.
- challenges such as creating schedules, writing and presenting stories and one-act plays, and presenting book reports in character.
- extending their reading experience with other books that support the theme, that were written by the same author, or that are the same genre.
- spending more time in independent exploration of libraries and media centers to create their own links to the books.

Second Language Learners

How can I use *BookFestival* with students who are working toward English proficiency? The quality literature and the ease with which students can manage the supportive materials make *BookFestival* ideal for language acquisition. All students are reading the rich literature and are collaborating and interacting with each other as they engage in reading and other activities, helping them to build self-esteem and to achieve literacy.

Learning Center

Listening Center

Classroom Organization

- **Print-rich environments** are those where children are surrounded with visuals that reinforce vocabulary and concepts. Help students write labels for desks, cabinets, and learning centers. Display children's work on walls and bulletin boards. If possible, tape children's work on mobiles hanging from the ceiling or on a clothesline strung across the room.

- **Learning centers** are ideal for group work. Copy onto index cards the Multicultural Connection, Vocabulary Strategies, and Connect Home and School notes from the teacher's Book-by-Book Notes. Place them in learning centers where students can share ideas and collaborate on meaningful activities. Set up an activity center using the Activity Cards and any materials students will need for the projects. The wide variety of multisensory and tactile activities will help to foster students' independent responses.

- **Listening centers** can provide all students access to the books. Ask students who need challenges to tape record books or parts of books for other students. Place the tapes in a listening center so all students may hear a story at their own pace and follow along in a book that they otherwise may be unable to read.

Partner Reading

Book Chat

Peer Interaction

- **Partner or paired reading** of students who are achieving English proficiency with more competent readers enables students to become familiar with the language as they read and reread the books aloud. Partners can work on the Reading Contract, setting goals that are realistic. Students may ask their partners about words they don't understand. A little guidance will help more competent readers to explain meanings.

- **Student collaboration** on Literature Masters and Activity Cards will promote oral language and concept development in a friendly, cooperative environment. Students may respond to the literature through a language mode—drama, drawing, retelling, or writing—suitable to their language proficiency.

- **Book Chats** will aid students' comprehension and self-concept as they verbalize their knowledge and excitement about the books they have read.

Assessment

How can I assess and evaluate students' progress? Your continuous evaluation of each student's progress will enable you to develop a truly individualized reading program. *BookFestival's* assessment suggestions and management forms help you to know each student's likes and dislikes, understanding, and prior knowledge so that you know what ongoing reading and relevant activities and projects students might benefit from at any given time.

Using Book-by-Book Notes

Book-by-Book Notes give suggestions for informal assessment of students' progress. In addition, your ongoing observations may include informal notes on the attitudes, interests, prior knowledge, preferences, and social relationships that you observe in the learning environment.

Book Chat *time allows you to assess students' understanding of the literature.*

Literature Masters and Activity Cards *provide samples for student portfolios.*

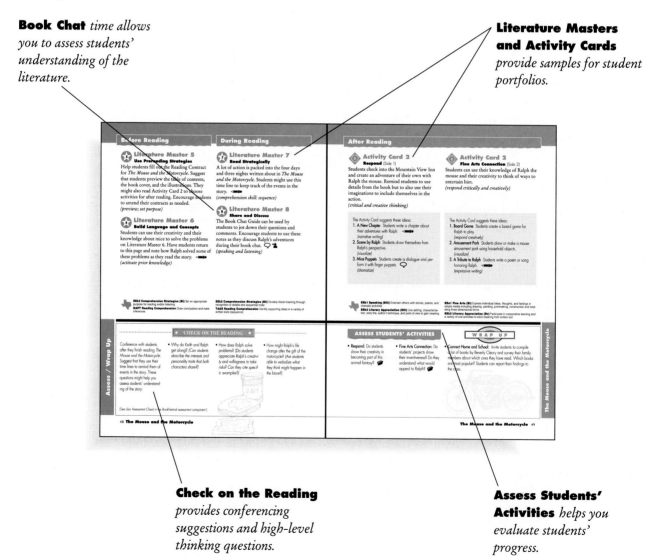

Check on the Reading *provides conferencing suggestions and high-level thinking questions.*

Assess Students' Activities *helps you evaluate students' progress.*

Using the Assessment Forms

Management forms for student assessment help you evaluate students' reading progress. Use the performance guidelines on the Assessment Checklist for informal assessment or as a way to assign grades for more formal evaluation.

Assessment Check Masters *let you check up on students' reading when you need to determine comprehension of each title read. (See BookFestival assessment components.)*

The Assessment Checklist *is a guide for checking students' overall development as you observe their reading, writing, work with the Literature Masters and Activity Cards, and contributions during Book Chats. (See Management Form #2.)*

The Conference Form *allows you to jot down your notes and suggestions about students as you meet with them to assess their reading progress and guide them in making literacy connections. (See Management Form #3.)*

Conference Tips

Student-teacher conferences enable you to discuss and monitor what the student is working on, how it is coming, and what he or she is planning to do next.

Peer conferences can be similar to the student-teacher conference or they can be a collaborative process in which two students talk out plans, try out their ideas in print, share reading and writing, receive and provide feedback, and proofread and edit each other's work.

Group conferences may take place during a regularly scheduled time, such as Book Chat time. As students discuss a book and listen to each other's comments, you can gain information about each student's reading comprehension and practice in using reading strategies.

Record Keeping

How can I keep track of the books, materials, and students' reading? *BookFestival* makes record keeping easy by providing the tools you and your students need to monitor students' reading and keep track of the books and materials. Since students share in the record keeping, keeping track of what they're doing is easier for you! These forms make it simple to fit *BookFestival* into any classroom.

Using the Student Portfolios

BookFestival portfolios are an easy way for students to keep track of books and materials at home or at school.

Student bookmarks

slip into students' portfolios and are ongoing reading logs that give students a sense of pride and accomplishment every time they check off the title of a book they've read. (See Management Form #4.)

Using the Record Keeping Forms

Management forms help you monitor students' reading, keep track of books, and encourage students to work independently and share responsibility for their reading.

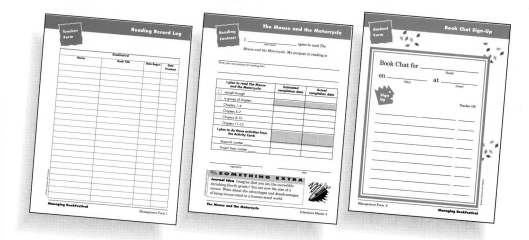

The Reading Record Log *is a great way to manage books and keep a record of students' reading. (See Management Form #1.)*

Reading Contract *Literature Masters are a running record of students' reading as well as a way to keep track of which activities they've completed. (See Literature Master section of this teacher's guide.)*

Book Chat Sign-Up *forms help students plan for book chats and help you keep track of students' progress as they read a book. (See Management Form #6.)*

Record Keeping Tips

- You might use one Record Keeping Log per student to maintain a list of students' reading during the year or number the copies of each book and make note of which students have those copies.

- Invite students to use the Something Extra ideas on their contracts to start a reading journal. Students might also use their journals to record ideas for book chats.

- You might want to use a checklist for keeping track of which Literature Masters students complete. Students can create their own checklists.

- Encourage students to design another bookmark for keeping track of other books they read throughout the year.

Home Involvement

How can *BookFestival* help me involve families in students' learning? Students tend to make a more determined effort to communicate clearly when their families share responsibility for their language development. Many families want to be involved in their child's education, and *BookFestival* is a great way to promote a home-school connection.

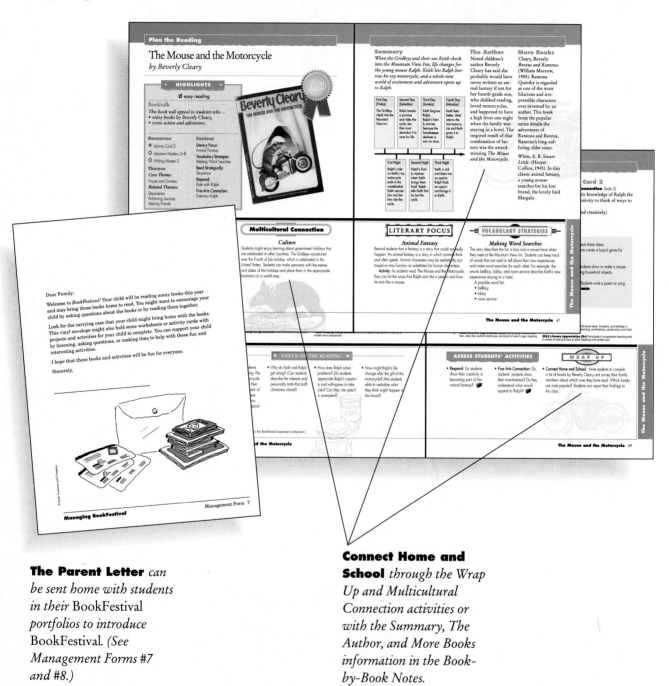

The Parent Letter *can be sent home with students in their* BookFestival *portfolios to introduce* BookFestival. *(See Management Forms #7 and #8.)*

Connect Home and School *through the Wrap Up and Multicultural Connection activities or with the Summary, The Author, and More Books information in the Book-by-Book Notes.*

Family Communication

You can keep family members informed when you
- summarize the week's activities in a newsletter.
- let families know when the child has done something well.
- videotape students' presentations and dramatizations. Send the video home with a different student each day.
- plan a family day when students may introduce their families to the learning environment.
- organize a series of young author days when a noted children's author speaks with students and families, or students share a book they have written.
- hold a read-a-thon when students and parents or other family members read aloud their favorite books.
- invite families to participate in the presentation of the *BookFestival* achievement awards.

School Connections

Family members helping at school might
- provide guidance for book projects.
- read aloud to students.
- listen to students read aloud.
- sit in on book chats.
- have one-to-one conferences with students about their reading.
- act as an audience for students' reading and writing accomplishments.
- assist in the book publishing process.
- start and continue a dialogue journal with students.

Home Connections

Family members helping at home might
- read with the child for a short time each day.
- talk about what the student did in school that day.
- listen to the child read aloud.
- read aloud to the child.
- talk about what the child has read or any questions the child wants to talk over.
- discuss the child's likes and dislikes about books, authors, or illustrators.
- share ideas, opinions, and experiences with the child.
- go to the library together and get another book by a favorite author or illustrator.

Multicultural Connections

How can I use *BookFestival* to develop cultural awareness in my students? *BookFestival* presents books that reflect the great cultural diversity of our country. Through both the books and the response activities, students appreciate their own cultural identities and make connections with people who are different from them in some ways but who share many of their values, goals, and experiences.

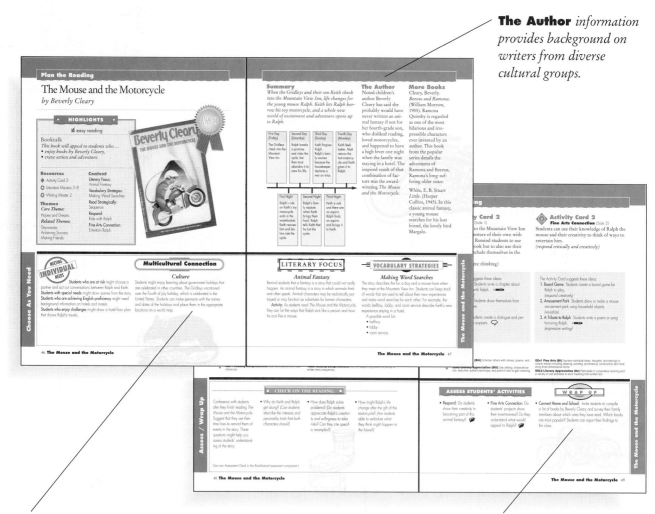

The Author *information provides background on writers from diverse cultural groups.*

Multicultural Connections *show how the literature lends itself to a discussion of key multicultural concepts and issues.*

Connect Home and School *wrap-up activities invite students to share ideas and concepts from the literature with their families.*

Integrating Multicultural Concepts

The Multicultural Connections in *BookFestival* give suggestions for activities that will help students acquire an understanding of these multicultural concepts in the context of the literature.

Culture, Ethnicity, and Related Concepts	**Acculturation:** the exchange and blending of cultural values and practices that occur between two ethnic groups
	Community culture: the unique culture of a community, consisting of shared values, language patterns, and behavior
	Cultural assimilation: a process by which members of a group take on the values and practices of another social group
	Culture: the way a group adapts to its physical, social, and metaphysical environment
	Ethnic diversity: the distinctive traits and traditions between and within ethnic groups in the U.S.
	Ethnic group: a microculture within the U.S. with a common history and traditions, often having some values and interests that differ from those of other groups in the U.S. Examples include Anglo-Saxon Protestants, Italian Americans, and Irish Americans.
	Ethnic minority group: a group of people—usually a numerical minority that exercises minimal political and economic power—with physical and/or cultural characteristics that make them easily identifiable. Examples include Vietnamese Americans, African Americans, and Jewish Americans.
Socialization and Related Concepts	**Discrimination:** the behavior arising from prejudice
	Ethnocentrism: the belief that one's own culture is superior to other cultures
	Prejudice: an attitude about others which is formed unfairly
	Racism: the belief that people of various races possess identifiable personality traits and levels of intelligence and that because of these traits some races are superior to others
	Self-concept: a person's beliefs about and evaluations of himself or herself
	Socialization: the process by which people learn what their society believes and how it behaves
	Values: the learned elements to which a group attaches great worth
Intercultural Communication and Related Concepts	**Communication:** a process by which someone receives and understands the words, actions, expressions, and images given by another person
	Environmental perception: the attitudes, feelings, and ideas that people have about their physical and cultural environment
	Historical bias: the fact that history is always a biased interpretation of events
	Intercultural communication: a process that is difficult to attain because people in different cultures often use similar words and images to mean different things
	Perception: the psychological process—often influenced by emotions, needs, expectations, and training—by which the brain uses data from the sense organs to make a meaningful whole
Power and Related Concepts	**Power:** the ability of a person or group to impose its will on others
	Social protest/resistance: the act of protesting social conditions, political policies, and economic practices that a group considers unjust
The Movement of Ethnic Groups	**Immigration:** the movement of an individual or group into a foreign country to live
	Migration: the movement of an individual or group from one place to another within a nation

SOURCE: *Teaching Strategies for Ethnic Studies*, Fifth Edition, by James A. Banks (Allyn and Bacon, 1991).

Glossary of Professional Terms

Assessment The collection of information and data gathering for the purpose of verifying strengths and weaknesses in achievement and informing teacher and student decision making.

Big Book Children's literature presented in an enlarged format; Big Books are used to model various reading strategies; children join in with the teacher for a shared reading experience.

Collaborative Learning A way of learning that allows peers to provide support through brainstorming, advising, clarifying, troubleshooting, editing and/or assessing one another's work.

Conferencing The stage in the reading or writing process when a teacher and one or more students meet for the purpose of evaluation of strategies.

Critical Thinking A reflective process by which a reader evaluates and judges the specific content in the context being read.

Cross-Curricular An instructional link between literature and other content areas.

Emergent Literacy The response to and interaction with language and print that allows children to gain understanding of the reading and writing process.

Flexible Grouping Homogeneous or heterogeneous temporary grouping based on need, interest, or task.

Genre Category of literature marked by a distinctive form or style, such as short story, fable, or biography.

Graphic Organizer A visual framework for organizing, comprehending, and synthesizing information; students can use graphic organizers to explore relationships between ideas.

Independent Reading A reading activity during which students read on their own, with little direct guidance from the teacher.

Informal Assessment and Evaluation Use of such materials as checklists, informal inventories, conferencing, and anecdotal records to assess student achievement.

Interactive Reading A way of looking at the reading process based on the belief that comprehension is dependent on what both the reader and the author bring to the text; sometimes referred to as Transactional Reading.

Literature Circle An opportunity for readers to talk about a book they have read and share their interpretations with others.

Mini-lesson A short lesson on a topic of current importance to the class or smaller groups.

Multicultural A term referring to the diverse range of cultures and subcultures representing various groups that make up a society.

Prior Knowledge Information a reader brings to a text about themes, ideas, words, purpose, conventions, and so on, that he or she draws upon during the reading process to construct meaning.

Reading/Writing Behavior The way in which children use language—by exploring, inventing, adapting, and creating—as readers and writers.

Response Written or oral transaction with a text or texts. Response can be personal, re-living the reading experience; critical, judging the content of the text; or creative, creating something new based on the reading experience.

Retelling A method used by students as a basis for recounting the selection and can be used as a basis for assessment or simply for purposes of sharing.

Shared Reading A process in which the teacher assumes first responsibility for reading a text. Through rereading with children, the teacher gradually withdraws support as children become more familiar with the text. Shared Reading can serve many purposes.

Supported Reading A reading activity in which the teacher provides support to students as needed.

SSR An acronym for Sustained Silent Reading. Students and the teacher silently read self-selected books during a regularly scheduled time.

Text Structure The organization of ideas in a written selection. Certain text features are inherent in a given text structure.

Trade Books Separately bound and published novels, plays, collections, or works of nonfiction.

Teacher Form

BookFestival			
Name	**Book Title**	**Date Begun**	**Date Finished**

Use this checklist as a class assessment form or as a record for one student.

Date	Student(s)																							

Reading

- Meets contract goals
- Displays sense of story
- Achieves set purpose
- Understands material

Literature Masters

- Completes masters
- Follows directions
- Spends appropriate time/effort
- Supports responses

Activity Cards

- Completes response activity
- Completes project
- Follows directions
- Spends appropriate time/effort
- Works cooperatively to plan and carry out
- Shows understanding of literature in response
- Shares project and how it relates to literature

Book Chats

- Comes to group prepared
- Participates in discussion
- Listens to other speakers
- Respects others' ideas
- Demonstrates understanding of literature

Writing

- Keeps to topic in prompt
- Presents information in organized manner
- Attends to mechanics

+ Strong performance   ✓ Adequate performance   − Needs help

Teacher Form

Student _____

Date	Book	Conference Notes

See "Check on the Reading" in Book-by-Book Notes for suggested conference questions.

Books I've Read

- ❏ The Adventures of Spider
- ❏ The Case of the Sabotaged School Play
- ❏ Esio Trot
- ❏ From Anna
- ❏ The Girl Who Loved the Wind
- ❏ Grandma Moses
- ❏ Kickle Snifters and Other Fearsome Critters
- ❏ The Mouse and the Motorcycle
- ❏ Night Markets
- ❏ Sarah, Plain and Tall
- ❏ Sidewalk Story
- ❏ Staying Nine
- ❏ Tales of a Fourth Grade Nothing
- ❏ There's a Boy in the Girls' Bathroom
- ❏ Willie Mays, Young Superstar

ScottForesman
BookFestival

ScottForesman
BookFestival

Name _____

Management Form 4

Managing BookFestival

Name _____

A Book Chat is a chance for you and other readers to talk about a book. You can share what you liked and disliked, what you questioned or wondered about, and what you thought about as you read.

Use these tips when you're ready for a Book Chat.

Setting Up a Book Chat

Pick a time and ask others to sign up if they want to "chat."
Find a place to talk.

Getting Ready for a Book Chat

As you read, use your Book Chat Guide or just jot down questions. Choose someone to lead the chat. The leader should have a plan or some questions that your group can follow as you talk:

What did you like about the book?
What did you wonder about? What questions did you have?
What in your own life or in another book does this book remind you of?

During a Book Chat

Encourage everyone to present their ideas.
Be sure you understand others' ideas. Ask questions. Reread as needed.
Listen and respect the ideas of others.

Book Chat for _____
(book)

on _____ at _____
(day) (time)

Sign Up

Teacher OK

_____ _____

_____ _____

_____ _____

_____ _____

_____ _____

_____ _____

_____ _____

_____ _____

Dear Family:

Welcome to *BookFestival!* Your child will be reading many books this year and may bring those books home to read. You might want to encourage your child by asking questions about the books or by reading them together.

Look for the carrying case that your child might bring home with the books. This vinyl envelope might also hold some worksheets or activity cards with projects and activities for your child to complete. You can support your child by listening, asking questions, or making time to help with these fun and interesting activities.

I hope that these books and activities will be fun for everyone.

Sincerely,

_____

Querida familia:

¡Bienvenidos al Festival del libro!—*BookFestival!*

Su hijo o hija va a leer muchos libros durante este año y quizá lleve algunos de ellos para leer en casa. Ustedes pueden alentarle en su lectura haciéndole preguntas acerca de los libros o leyéndolos juntos.

Busque la bolsa que su hijo o hija quizá lleve a la casa con los libros. Esta bolsa plástica a veces contiene hojas de trabajo o tarjetas de actividades y proyectos que su hijo o hija debe completar. Ustedes pueden estimularle oyéndole, haciéndole preguntas or ayudándole con estas actividades interesantes y divertidas.

Espero que todos se diviertan con estos libros y actividades.

Atentamente,

Let's Celebrate!

_____
(Name)

is finished reading

_____
(Title)

and did a terrific job on

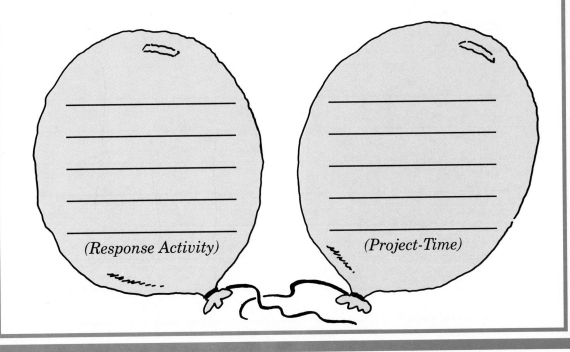

_____
_____
_____
_____
_____
(Response Activity)

_____
_____
_____
_____
_____
(Project-Time)

Student Review

of

★ _____ ★

(book title)

by

_____

(your name)

Overall I give this book _____

(1–5 stars)

Reasons to
read this book: _____

_____

_____

_____

_____

_____

_____

_____

BookFestival at a Glance

Title	Book-by-Book Notes	Literature Masters	Texas Writing Practice Masters
The Girl Who Loved the Wind	pages 42–45	1–4	1
The Mouse and the Motorcycle	pages 46–49	5–8	2
There's a Boy in the Girls' Bathroom	pages 50–53	9–12	3
Night Markets	pages 54–57	13–16	4
Sidewalk Story	pages 58–61	17–20	5
Tales of a Fourth Grade Nothing	pages 62–65	21–24	6
Staying Nine	pages 66–69	25–28	7
Willie Mays: Young Superstar	pages 70–73	29–32	8
Esio Trot	pages 74–77	33–36	9
Sarah, Plain and Tall	pages 78–81	37–40	10
Grandma Moses: Painter of Rural America	pages 82–85	41–44	11
Kickle Snifters and Other Fearsome Critters	pages 86–89	45–48	12
The Case of the Sabotaged School Play	pages 90–93	49–52	13
From Anna	pages 94–97	53–56	14
The Adventures of Spider	pages 98–101	57–60	15

The Girl Who Loved the Wind
by Jane Yolen

• HIGHLIGHTS •

☑ average reading

Booktalk

This book will appeal to students who...
- *enjoy picture books,*
- *appreciate folk tales.*

Resources

◆ Activity Card 1

✪ Literature Masters 1–4

✪ Writing Master 1

Themes

Core Theme:

Hopes and Dreams

Related Themes:

Fantasy
Wishes Come True
Imagination

Content

Literary Focus:
Setting

Vocabulary Strategies:
Descriptive Words

Read Strategically:
Summarize

Respond:
Danina's Decision

Fine Arts Connection:
Go with the Wind

Choose As You Need

MEETING INDIVIDUAL NEEDS

Students who are at risk might work in a group, prepare, and read the book aloud. 🧍🧍🧍🧍 💬
Students with special needs might need assistance with difficult vocabulary words.
Students who are achieving English proficiency might benefit from listening to the story read by a peer. 🗨🧍
Students who enjoy challenges might prepare and present the story to a younger class.

Multicultural Connection

Culture

People all over the world enjoy storytelling. Students could look through folk tale collections for traditional stories from different parts of the world. Students could also ask their relatives and neighbors about favorite childhood stories. Did some of the stories originate in other countries? Students could learn these tales and retell them in class. 💬 🗨🧍

Summary

Long ago and far away a wealthy merchant shuts his beloved daughter Danina away from all the sadness in the world. When Danina hears the wind whisper to her of life in the world outside her father's house, she longs to experience it.

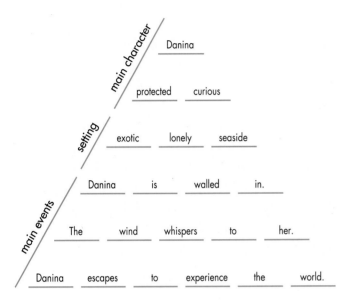

The Author

Prolific author Jane Yolen notes that a class of sixth graders once asked why so many of her books deal with walls. Since she had never noticed that walls were a recurring image in her work, she and the students reflected on it together. She concluded that for her, walls represent the difference between freedom and imprisonment, or between comfort and the frightening but real world outside. Books like *The Girl Who Loved the Wind*, *The Seventh Mandarin*, and *The Seeing Stick* are about the world that exists "beyond the wall."

More Books

Yolen, Jane. *Sleeping Ugly*. (Coward, McCann & McGeoghegan, 1981). In this story, Jane Yolen gives traditional fairy tales an unusual twist. A young prince chooses good-hearted Plain Jane instead of the beautiful, spoiled Princess Miserella.

McDermott, Gerald. *Arrow to the Sun*. (Puffin, 1977). A boy leaves his home on Earth to search for his father, the Lord of the Sun, in this Pueblo Indian myth.

LITERARY FOCUS

Setting

Remind students that setting is when and where a story happens. The setting can sometimes cause problems for the characters in a story.

Activity: As students read *The Girl Who Loved the Wind*, have them write down clues from the text and the illustrations that describe the setting. How does the setting affect Danina?

VOCABULARY STRATEGIES

Classifying Descriptive Words

Jane Yolen uses wonderful descriptions in *The Girl Who Loved the Wind*, with strong adjectives and verbs. For example, the verbs *whirled*, *sough*, *whipped*, and *rustle* describe the wind. Students can keep track of powerful descriptive words.

A possible word list:
- whirled—verb
- sough—verb
- dainty—adjective
- silken—adjective

Literature Master 1
Use Prereading Strategies

Help students fill out the Reading Contract for *The Girl Who Loved the Wind*. Suggest students preview the illustrations and the book jacket. They might also read Activity Card 1 to select activities for after reading. Students should feel free to amend their contracts as needed.
(preview; set purpose)

 Literature Master 2
Build Language and Concepts

Students reflect upon what makes them happy. Using Literature Master 2 as a starting point, students can share their personal ideas about happiness.
(activate prior knowledge)

 Literature Master 3
Read Strategically

The Girl Who Loved the Wind is a short but thought-provoking folk tale. Literature Master 3 invites students to fill in a "story triangle" that briefly describes the setting and summarizes the plot.
(comprehension skill: summarize)

 Literature Master 4
Share and Discuss

Encourage open response after students have read *The Girl Who Loved the Wind*. Literature Master 4 provides starter questions for literature groups or your conferences with students. Students can also use the Book Chat Guide to jot down questions and comments about the plot, characters, and illustrations in the story.
(speaking and listening)

EEk1 Speaking (Bii) Describe personal ideas, feelings, and experiences
EEk2 Comprehension Strategies (Bi) Set an appropriate purpose for reading and/or listening

EEk2 Comprehension Strategies (Bii) Develop literal meaning through recognition of details and sequential order
TAAS Reading Comprehension Summarize a variety of written texts

Assess / Wrap Up

■ CHECK ON THE READING ■

Conference with students after they finish reading *The Girl Who Loved the Wind*. These questions might help you assess students' understanding of the story:

- Why does Danina's father keep her away from the world? *(Do students realize that he is overprotective? that he thinks he can shelter her from all sadness?)*

- Why does the wind make Danina restless? *(Do students understand that she is curious about the world outside her walls?)*

- Do you agree with Danina's choice? Explain why or why not. *(Are students able to express an opinion and support it with reasons?)*

(See also Assessment Check in the BookFestival assessment component.)

Activity Card 1
Respond (Side 1)

Students put themselves in Danina's place and express how she feels about her situation. *(critical and creative thinking)*

The Activity Card suggests these ideas:
1. **Write a Letter** Students write a letter from Danina to her father explaining why she left home with the wind.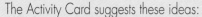
   (expressive writing)
2. **Keep a Diary** Students write diary entries from Danina's point of view.
   (narrative writing)
3. **Have a Talk Show** Students hold an interview between Danina and her father.
   (dramatize)

EEk2 Literary Appreciation (Diii) Use setting, characterization, story line, author's technique, and point of view to gain meaning
EEk3 Writing (Share Products) (E) Share products of composition in a variety of ways

 Activity Card 1
Fine Arts Connection (Side 2)

Students can use their imaginations to continue the story of Danina and the wind. *(respond creatively)*

The Activity Card suggests these ideas:
1. **Make a Scroll** Students illustrate the adventures of Danina and the wind.
   (visualize)
2. **Write a Ballad** Students write and perform a song about Danina and the wind.
   (expressive writing)
3. **Perform a Skit** Students plan and perform a pantomime about Danina's experiences.
   (dramatize)

EEk2 Literary Appreciation (Dv) Participate in cooperative learning and a variety of oral activities to elicit meaning from written text
EEe3 Fine Arts (B) Dramatize literary selections using shadow play, pantomime, creative dialogue, improvisation, characterization, and puppetry

ASSESS STUDENTS' ACTIVITIES

- **Respond:**
  Do students show that they understand Danina's feelings?

- **Fine Arts Connection:**
  Do students' projects reflect a creative continuation of the folk tale?

 **WRAP UP**

- **Connect Home and School:** Invite students to take the book home to read to a younger relative or neighbor. How does the person react to the story?

The Girl Who Loved the Wind

The Mouse and the Motorcycle
by Beverly Cleary

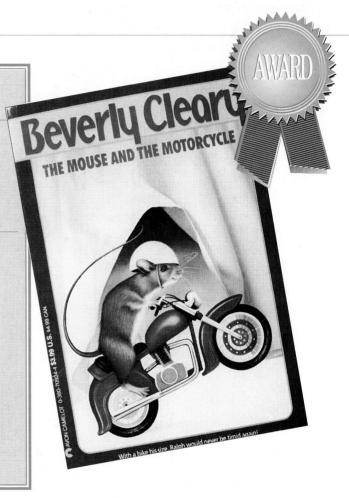

• HIGHLIGHTS •

☑ easy reading

Booktalk

This book will appeal to students who ...
- *enjoy books by Beverly Cleary,*
- *crave action and adventure.*

Resources

◆ Activity Card 2

✪ Literature Masters 5–8

✪ Writing Master 2

Themes

Core Theme:
Hopes and Dreams

Related Themes:
Discoveries
Achieving Success
Making Friends

Content

Literary Focus:
Animal Fantasy

Vocabulary Strategies:
Making Word Searches

Read Strategically:
Sequence

Respond:
Ride with Ralph

Fine Arts Connection:
Entertain Ralph

MEETING INDIVIDUAL NEEDS

Students who are at risk might choose a partner and act out conversations between Ralph and Keith. **Students with special needs** might draw scenes from the story. **Students who are achieving English proficiency** might need background information on hotels and motels. **Students who enjoy challenges** might draw a hotel floor plan that shows Ralph's travels. ♦♦

Multicultural Connection

Culture

Students might enjoy learning about government holidays that are celebrated in other countries. The Gridleys vacationed over the Fourth of July holiday, which is celebrated in the United States. Students can make pennants with the names and dates of the holidays and place them in the appropriate locations on a world map.

Choose As You Need

Summary

When the Gridleys and their son Keith check into the Mountain View Inn, life changes for the young mouse Ralph. Keith lets Ralph borrow his toy motorcycle, and a whole new world of excitement and adventure opens up to Ralph.

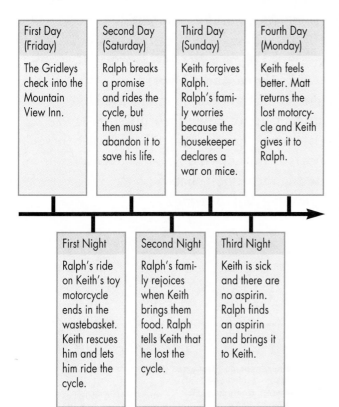

First Day (Friday)
The Gridleys check into the Mountain View Inn.

Second Day (Saturday)
Ralph breaks a promise and rides the cycle, but then must abandon it to save his life.

Third Day (Sunday)
Keith forgives Ralph. Ralph's family worries because the housekeeper declares a war on mice.

Fourth Day (Monday)
Keith feels better. Matt returns the lost motorcycle and Keith gives it to Ralph.

First Night
Ralph's ride on Keith's toy motorcycle ends in the wastebasket. Keith rescues him and lets him ride the cycle.

Second Night
Ralph's family rejoices when Keith brings them food. Ralph tells Keith that he lost the cycle.

Third Night
Keith is sick and there are no aspirin. Ralph finds an aspirin and brings it to Keith.

The Author

Noted children's author Beverly Cleary has said she probably would have never written an animal fantasy if not for her fourth-grade son, who disliked reading, loved motorcycles, and happened to have a high fever one night when the family was staying in a hotel. The inspired result of that combination of factors was the award-winning *The Mouse and the Motorcycle*.

More Books

Cleary, Beverly. *Beezus and Ramona*. (William Morrow, 1955). Ramona Quimby is regarded as one of the most hilarious and irrepressible characters ever invented by an author. This book from the popular series details the adventures of Ramona and Beezus, Ramona's long-suffering older sister.

White, E. B. *Stuart Little*. (Harper Collins, 1945). In this classic animal fantasy, a young mouse searches for his lost friend, the lovely bird Margalo.

LITERARY FOCUS

Animal Fantasy

Remind students that a fantasy is a story that could not really happen. An animal fantasy is a story in which animals think and often speak. Animal characters may be realistically portrayed or may function as substitutes for human characters.

Activity: As students read *The Mouse and the Motorcycle*, they can list the ways that Ralph acts like a person and how he acts like a mouse.

VOCABULARY STRATEGIES

Making Word Searches

The story describes the fun a boy and a mouse have when they meet at the Mountain View Inn. Students can keep track of words that are used to tell about their new experiences and make word searches for each other. For example, the words *bellboy*, *lobby*, and *room service* describe Keith's new experience staying in a hotel.

A possible word list:
- bellboy
- lobby
- room service

Literature Master 5
Use Prereading Strategies

Help students fill out the Reading Contract for *The Mouse and the Motorcycle*. Suggest that students preview the table of contents, the book cover, and the illustrations. They might also read Activity Card 2 to choose activities for after reading. Encourage students to amend their contracts as needed.
(preview; set purpose)

Literature Master 6
Build Language and Concepts

Students can use their creativity and their knowledge about mice to solve the problems on Literature Master 6. Have students return to this page and note how Ralph solved some of these problems as they read the story.
(activate prior knowledge)

Literature Master 7
Read Strategically

A lot of action is packed into the four days and three nights written about in *The Mouse and the Motorcycle*. Students might use this time line to keep track of the events in the story.
(comprehension skill: sequence)

Literature Master 8
Share and Discuss

The Book Chat Guide can be used by students to jot down their questions and comments. Encourage students to use these notes as they discuss Ralph's adventures during their book chat.
(speaking and listening)

EEk2 Comprehension Strategies (Bi) Set an appropriate purpose for reading and/or listening
NAPT Reading Comprehension Draw conclusions and make inferences

EEk2 Comprehension Strategies (Bii) Develop literal meaning through recognition of details and sequential order
TAAS Reading Comprehension Identify supporting ideas in a variety of written texts (sequence)

Assess / Wrap Up

■ CHECK ON THE READING ■

Conference with students after they finish reading *The Mouse and the Motorcycle*. Suggest that they use their time lines to remind them of events in the story. These questions might help you assess students' understanding of the story:

• Why do Keith and Ralph get along? *(Can students describe the interests and personality traits that both characters share?)*

• How does Ralph solve problems? *(Do students appreciate Ralph's creativity and willingness to take risks? Can they cite specific examples?)*

• How might Ralph's life change after the gift of the motorcycle? *(Are students able to verbalize what they think might happen in the future?)*

(See also Assessment Check in the BookFestival assessment component.)

Activity Card 2
Respond (Side 1)

Students check into the Mountain View Inn and create an adventure of their own with Ralph the mouse. Remind students to use details from the book but to also use their imaginations to include themselves in the action.

(critical and creative thinking)

 Activity Card 2
Fine Arts Connection (Side 2)

Students can use their knowledge of Ralph the mouse and their creativity to think of ways to entertain him.

(respond critically and creatively)

The Activity Card suggests these ideas:

1. **A New Chapter** Students write a chapter about their adventures with Ralph. ◀▬█▬▷
(narrative writing)

2. **Scene by Ralph** Students draw themselves from Ralph's perspective.
(visualize)

3. **Mice Puppets** Students create a dialogue and perform it with finger puppets. 🗩
(dramatize)

The Activity Card suggests these ideas:

1. **Board Game** Students create a board game for Ralph to play.
(respond creatively)

2. **Amusement Park** Students draw or make a mouse amusement park using household objects.
(visualize)

3. **A Tribute to Ralph** Students write a poem or song honoring Ralph. ◀▬█▬▷
(expressive writing)

EEk1 Speaking (Biii) Entertain others with stories, poems, and dramatic activities
EEk2 Literary Appreciation (Diii) Use setting, characterization, story line, author's technique, and point of view to gain meaning

EEe1 Fine Arts (Bi) Express individual ideas, thoughts, and feelings in simple media including drawing, painting, printmaking, construction and modeling three-dimensional forms
EEk2 Literary Appreciation (Dv) Participate in cooperative learning and a variety of oral activities to elicit meaning from written text

---

ASSESS STUDENTS' ACTIVITIES

- **Respond:** Do students show their creativity in becoming part of this animal fantasy?

- **Fine Arts Connection:** Do students' projects show their inventiveness? Do they understand what would appeal to Ralph? 📓

WRAP UP

- **Connect Home and School:** Invite students to compile a list of books by Beverly Cleary and survey their family members about which ones they have read. Which books are most popular? Students can report their findings to the class.

There's a Boy in the Girls' Bathroom
by Louis Sachar

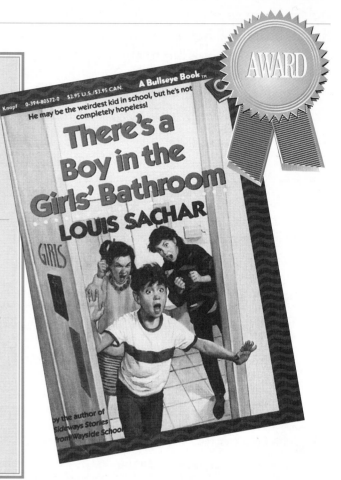

• HIGHLIGHTS •

☑ average reading

Booktalk

This book will appeal to students who . . .
- *enjoy realistic fiction about school,*
- *may sometimes feel they don't fit in.*

Resources

◆ Activity Card 3

✪ Literature Masters 9–12

✪ Writing Master 3

Themes

Core Theme:
School Stories

Related Themes:
Dreamers and Achievers
Friendship

Content

Literary Focus:
Realistic Fiction

Vocabulary Strategies:
Illustrating "Bradley" Scenes

Read Strategically:
Details and Facts

Respond:
Friends of Bradley

Social Studies Connection:
Help New Students

MEETING INDIVIDUAL NEEDS

Students who are at risk might benefit from writing a one-sentence summary after reading each chapter.

Students with special needs might benefit from listening to the story on a tape made by another student. ᵐ🧑

Students who are achieving English proficiency might benefit from reading the dialogue aloud with a partner. 👫

Students who enjoy challenges might want to act out a scene between Bradley and Carla Davis. 👪👪

Multicultural Connection

Socialization

Point out that Bradley didn't know what he was supposed to do at a birthday party. Ask students to remember a time when they were in a situation where they weren't sure what to do or how to act. How did students feel? How did they figure out what to do? What would they tell someone else who was facing the same situation? Students can share their experiences in a group discussion. 👪👪👪

Choose As You Need

Summary

Bradley Chalkers suffers from low self-esteem. His only friends are the small glass animals in his collection, and he doesn't have a clue about how to succeed in school. Carla Davis, the new counselor at Red Hill School, helps him be successful in both his personal and academic life.

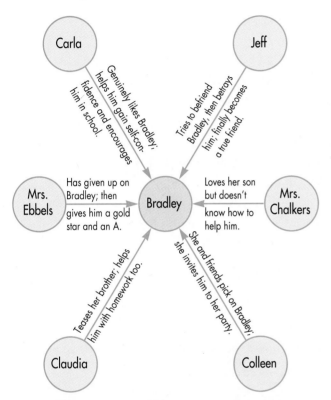

The Author

Although *There's a Boy in the Girls' Bathroom* has been Louis Sachar's most popular book, he had a difficult time finding a publisher after he wrote it. Sachar (pronounced sak´ər) has written a number of other books for children, including *Sideways Stories from Wayside School* and *Johnny's in the Basement.*

More Books

Sachar, Louis. *Sideways Stories from Wayside School.* (Alfred A. Knopf, 1978). Wayside School is not like any school you've ever seen, and neither are the students! These silly stories are full of unexpected events.

Park, Barbara. *The Kid in the Red Jacket.* (Alfred A. Knopf, 1987). When his family moves to Massachusetts, ten-year-old Howard is not sure he's going to like his new house or his new school.

LITERARY FOCUS

Realistic Fiction

Remind students that realistic fiction describes events that could really happen. The characters are like real people, and the things that happen in the story could happen in real life.

Activity: As students read *There's a Boy in the Girls' Bathroom,* suggest that they compare the students and teachers at Red Hill School with those in their own school. They might enjoy writing a piece of realistic fiction based on a true story from an experience at their own school. ◄▬▬ᴮ

VOCABULARY STRATEGIES

Illustrating "Bradley" Scenes

Bradley Chalkers doesn't think very highly of himself. He's always in trouble and he's not very successful in school. He uses words and phrases, such as *enemy, fighting,* and *bad boy* to describe himself. Students can keep track of related words and phrases and use them to illustrate a scene from Bradley's life. ◄▬▬ᴮ

A possible word list:
- enemy
- fighting
- bad boy

Literature Master 9
Use Prereading Strategies

Help students fill out the Reading Contract for *There's a Boy in the Girls' Bathroom.* Suggest students preview the illustrations and text on the book covers as well as the first few paragraphs of the book. They might also skim Activity Card 3 to select activities for after reading.
(preview; set purpose)

 Literature Master 10
Build Language and Concepts

Pairs of students could use the problem/solution game board on Literature Master 10 to discuss problems they might encounter in school and possible solutions. Encourage students to add ideas as they read *There's a Boy in the Girls' Bathroom.*
(activate prior knowledge)

 Literature Master 11
Read Strategically

The characters in *There's a Boy in the Girls' Bathroom* relate to each other in different ways at different times. The chart on Literature Master 11 can help students keep track of the relationships among the characters in the book.
(comprehension skill: details and facts)

 Literature Master 12
Share and Discuss

Encourage open response from students when they discuss *There's a Boy in the Girls' Bathroom.* Literature Master 12 suggests some questions for discussion during a book chat or a conference. Students can add their own questions and comments about the story.
(speaking and listening)

EEk2 Comprehension Stretegies (Bi) Set an appropriate purpose for reading and/or listening
TAAS Reading Comprehension Perceives relationships and recognizes outcomes in a variety of written texts (Predict)

EEk2 Literary Appreciation (Diii) Use setting, characterization, story line, author's technique, and point of view to gain meaning
NAPT Reading Comprehension Infer the traits, feelings, and motivations of characters

■ **CHECK ON THE READING** ■

Meet with students to discuss the book after they finish reading it. They might use their relationship chart to remember events in the story. These questions might help you assess students' understanding of the story:

• How does Carla Davis affect the lives of the students at Red Hill School? *(Do students recognize that she has helped students, most notably Bradley, to change their behavior for the better?)*

• How does Bradley change by the end of the story? *(Do students recognize that by the end of the story, Bradley feels better about himself and can treat others in a friendlier way?)*

• Is *There's a Boy in the Girls' Bathroom* realistic? Why or why not? *(Can students verbalize their opinions and support them with facts from the story and real life?)*

(See also *Assessment Check* in the *BookFestival* assessment component.)

Activity Card 3
Respond (Side 1)

The Activity Card suggests these ideas: Students imagine themselves in Mrs. Ebbel's class and try to befriend Bradley. Remind students to use details from the book and also their own school experiences in their responses.
(critical and creative thinking)

The Activity Card suggests these ideas:
1. **Write a Reply** Students write a reply to an advice column letter from Bradley.
   (persuasive writing)
2. **Make a Collage** Students create a collage depicting what will make Bradley happy.
   (visualize)
3. **Give a Gift** Students draw a gift for Bradley and explain why it is "from the heart."
   (visualize; informative writing)

 EEk3 Writing (Select Topics) (Aii) Gather information and ideas from a variety of sources including personal experiences and literature
EEk3 Writing (Draft) (Bv) Write in a variety of literary forms

 ## Activity Card 3
Social Studies Connection (Side 2)

Students can create a new student handbook as they explore the difficulties new students face, formulate a code of student behavior, and research facts about the school.
(synthesize information)

The Activity Card suggests these ideas:
1. **Interviews** Students gather information about problems new students had when they started at their school.
   (organize information)
2. **Cartoons** Students draw the do's and don'ts of student behavior.
   (visualize)
3. **School Facts** Students research and write about school history, famous students, and so on.
   (use reference sources; informative writing)

EEk3 Writing (Share Products) (E) Share products of composition in a variety of ways
EEe1 Social Studies (C) Explain how groups influence individual behavior

ASSESS STUDENTS' ACTIVITIES

- **Respond:** Do students empathize with Bradley's situation? Do they make positive suggestions for Bradley?

- **Social Studies Connection:** Do the new student handbooks provide helpful information? Are they entertaining and interesting to read?

- **Connect Home and School:** Do parents feel counselors or computers are more important to have at school? Have students poll their parents and graph the findings. Discuss the results.

 **Boy in the Girls' Bathroom**

Night Markets
by Joshua Horwitz

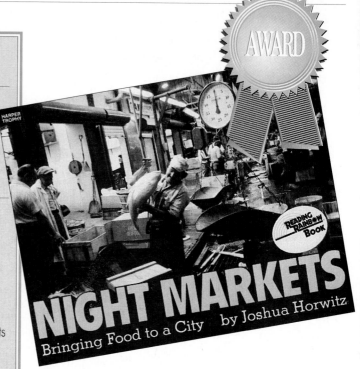

NIGHT MARKETS
Bringing Food to a City   by Joshua Horwitz

• HIGHLIGHTS •

☑ easy reading

Booktalk

This book will appeal to students who...
- *are interested in food,*
- *love nonfiction about people and places.*

Resources

◆ Activity Card 4

✪ Literature Masters 13–16

✪ Writing Master 4

Themes

Core Theme:

Learning Outside of School

Related Themes:

Transportation
Food
Learning About the World

Content

Literary Focus:
Photo Essay

Vocabulary Strategies:
Food Words

Read Strategically:
Main Idea; Details and Facts

Respond:
Be a Tour Guide

Social Studies Connection:
Sell Your State

Choose As You Need

MEETING INDIVIDUAL NEEDS

Students who are at risk might be encouraged to preview the book paying special attention to the photographs. They can predict what they think the text will describe and check by reading.

Students with special needs might enjoy discussing the processes shown in the text. 💬 "🧍

Students who are achieving English proficiency might benefit from discussion about how food moves from farms to stores before reading. 💬 "🧍

Students who enjoy challenges might trace the path of a single food from farm to supermarket.

Multicultural Connection

Acculturation

Nowhere do ethnic groups exchange cultural values and practices more than in food! Students might enjoy tracing a favorite food back to the people who first ate and enjoyed it. How do people enjoy this food today? Students might share what they find out by showing their information on an illustrated time line. ✏️▬▬▷ 🏃🏃🏃🏃

Summary

Night Markets *documents the activities at a variety of wholesale markets that supply meat, fish, produce, baked goods, and dairy products to New York City.*

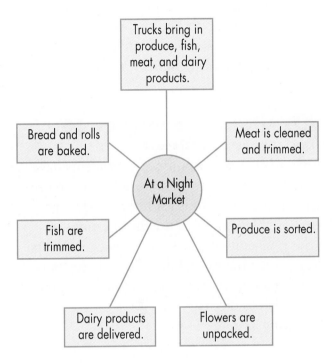

Trucks bring in produce, fish, meat, and dairy products.

Meat is cleaned and trimmed.

Bread and rolls are baked.

At a Night Market

Fish are trimmed.

Produce is sorted.

Dairy products are delivered.

Flowers are unpacked.

The Author

Joshua Horwitz works in film and video in New York City. *Doll Hospital* was the first photo essay he wrote and illustrated for children. *Doll Hospital* describes a "hospital" in mid-town Manhattan where a "doctor" restores dolls from all over the world.

More Books

Cole, Joanna. *Cars and How They Go.* (Crowell, 1983). This book makes it fun to understand cars and engines.

Arnosky, Jim. *Secrets of a Wildlife Watcher.* (Lothrop/Beech Tree, 1983). The author/artist explains when, where, and how to look for animals in the wild.

LITERARY FOCUS

Photo Essay

Remind students that illustrations can provide details and facts. Discuss the information the photos in *Night Markets* provide. How would the tone and mood of the book be different if the author had chosen to illustrate *Night Markets* with drawings instead of photos? (Photographs make the text more realistic, and some styles of art might communicate a different feeling.)

Activity: Suggest that students cut out pictures from old magazines and newspapers and use them to create a photo essay of their own.

VOCABULARY STRATEGIES

Classifying Food Words

Students might enjoy listing all the names of foods they come across in *Night Markets*. Suggest that they then decide on categories for their words, for example, fruits, vegetables, meats. Then they can share their classifying schemas.

A possible word list:

- bagel
- lox
- asparagus
- veal

Night Markets

Literature Master 13
Use Prereading Strategies

Help students fill out the Reading Contract for *Night Markets*. Students might preview the book in order to set their purpose for reading. Suggest that they look over the Activity Card and plan the activities they would like to do. Point out that the contract is intended to help them plan their reading of *Night Markets*. Students should feel free to amend their contracts as needed.
(preview; set purpose)

 ### Literature Master 14
Build Language and Concepts

Groups of students might work together to complete the activity. Students might brainstorm their ideas, list them in order, and then work together to complete their diagrams.
(activate prior knowledge)

 ### Literature Master 15
Read Strategically

Literature Master 15 directs students to record details from *Night Markets* they then use to figure out the main idea. Some students may want to group details and write more than one main idea statement. The goal is for students to see the big idea(s) of the book.
(comprehension skill: main idea; details and facts)

 ### Literature Master 16
Share and Discuss

Encourage open response after students have read *Night Markets*. Literature Master 16 provides starter questions for literature groups. Or you might want to use the questions in your own conference with students. Students might keep the Book Chat Guide in the book, making it convenient to jot down questions they wish to discuss.
(speaking and listening)

EEk2 Comprehension Strategies (Bi) Set an appropriate purpose for reading and/or listening
NAPT Reading Comprehension Draw conclusions and make inferences

EEk2 Comprehension Strategies (Biii) Develop global meaning by analyzing text to identify main idea and to develop a summary
NAPT Reading Comprehension Identify the main idea or topic of a passage or portion of a passage

Assess / Wrap Up

■ CHECK ON THE READING ■

Conference with students after they finish reading *Night Markets*. Suggest they use their main idea and detail organizer to remind them of what they have read. These questions might help assess understanding of the book:

• What are the night markets? *(Do students understand that the book tells about some of the activities at the wholesale markets in New York City during the night?)*

• What are some of the jobs people do at the night markets? *(Do students mention a range of jobs, such as trimming meat, sorting flowers, delivering dairy products, and baking bread?)*

• Pick a market and pretend you are there. What do you see, hear, and smell? *(Do students mention being at the flower market, the fish market, or one of the bakeries? Do they use words that describe smells, sights, and sounds?)*

(See also Assessment Check in the BookFestival assessment component.)

Activity Card 4
Respond (Side 1)

Activity Card 4 provides a prompt for students' personal response to *Night Markets*. Students are to imagine they are tour guides for the markets in New York City. Students can be creative in the details they add, but added details should reflect the spirit of *Night Markets*.
(critical and creative thinking)

The Activity Card suggests these ideas:

1. **Give a Talk** Students give a talk as the tour guide, telling what the class will see on the field trip.
(share information)

2. **Create an Ad** Students write an ad that advertises the tour of the markets.
(persuasive writing)

3. **Write an Article** Students write a newspaper article that describes the activities of the markets in New York City.
(informative writing)

 EEk1 Speaking (Bv) Share information
EEk2 Literary Appreciation (Dv) Participate in cooperative learning and a variety of oral activities to elicit meaning from written text

 Activity Card 4
Social Studies Connection (Side 2)

Students research the products their state grows, collects, or produces. Such information can be found in most encyclopedias and in nonfiction books on individual states. You might want to assign activities to individual students or groups.
(use reference sources)

The Activity Card suggests these ideas:

1. **Draw a Map** Students draw a map and include the products of the state.
(maps)

2. **Make a List** Students list and classify state products.
(lists)

3. **Write an Article** Students write an article telling the journey a product takes from his or her state to where it is used.
(narrative writing)

EEk2 Study Strategies (Ciii) Locate information using the dictionary, encyclopedia, and other library references including database searching strategies
EEe2 Social Studies (A) Explain the importance of economic interdependence

ASSESS STUDENTS' ACTIVITIES

- **Respond:** Do students show an understanding of the activities at various wholesale markets in New York City?

- **Social Studies Connection:** Can students locate information about their state and present it in an understandable way?

WRAP UP

- **Connect Home and School:** Invite students to investigate the various ways foods are available. On a trip to the supermarket with a parent, students might see how many ways a food such as apples is available. Are apples available fresh? frozen? dried? processed in pies and cakes? Students might report back to the class about what they have learned.

Sidewalk Story
by Sharon Bell Mathis

☑ easy reading

Booktalk
This book will appeal to students who ...
- *like stories about friends,*
- *like to read about city kids.*

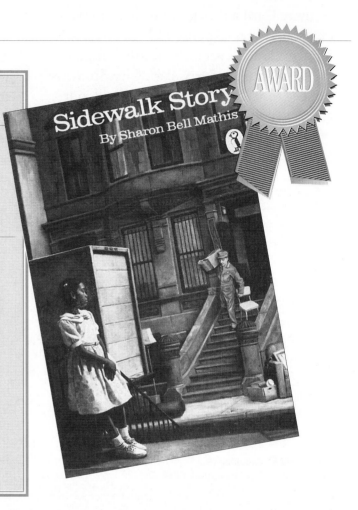

Resources
◆ Activity Card 5

⭐ Literature Masters 17–20

⭐ Writing Master 5

Themes
Core Theme:
Caring

Related Themes:
Friends and Families
Wishes Come True
Making It Happen

Content
Literary Focus:
Theme

Vocabulary Strategies:
City Words

Read Strategically:
Draw Conclusions

Respond:
Step into the Story

Math Connection:
Money Matters

Choose As You Need

MEETING INDIVIDUAL NEEDS

Students who are at risk might enjoy reading *Sidewalk Story* aloud with a partner. 👬

Students with special needs might use simple paper cutouts of the characters to retell the story. 💬

Students who are achieving English proficiency might need explanation of some of the city services described in the story.

Students who enjoy challenges might enjoy dramatizing scenes from the story. 💬

Multicultural Connection

Socialization

Where do children learn how to behave toward others? Remind students that adults teach children by demonstration, and that other institutions, such as schools and churches, also provide guidance in beliefs and behaviors. Students might discuss the role models of the adults in *Sidewalk Story*. What messages are they communicating to the children? 💬 🗣️

Summary

Lilly Etta's best friend's family is being evicted. She decides she is the only who can help them.

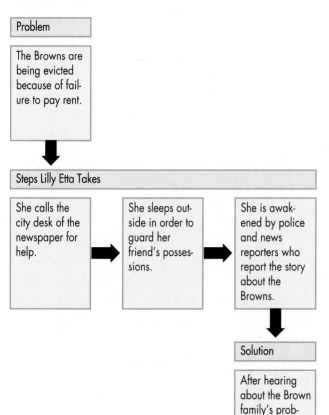

Problem

The Browns are being evicted because of failure to pay rent.

Steps Lilly Etta Takes

She calls the city desk of the newspaper for help.

She sleeps outside in order to guard her friend's possessions.

She is awakened by police and news reporters who report the story about the Browns.

Solution

After hearing about the Brown family's problems, people in the community offer help.

The Author

Sharon Bell Mathis recalls that as much as she read as a child, her mother read more! She remembers seeing her mother with a book at all hours of the day. Ms. Mathis recalls that sharing books and later her own writing with her mother was something very special. For her books, Ms. Mathis has earned the respect of critics outside her family as well.

More Books

Keller, Beverly. *No Beasts! No Children!* (HarperTrophy, 1988). When the landlord discovers that Desdemona's family has three large dogs, he tells them to get rid of the dogs or get out! Desdemona takes up the challenge to change the landlord's mind.

Monjo, F. N. *The One Bad Thing About Father.* (HarperTrophy, 1970). The one bad thing is that father is the President of the United States! Monjo has created a delightful biography of the Theodore Roosevelt family in the White House.

LITERARY FOCUS

Theme

Remind students that authors often want to give readers a message, in addition to telling a good story. Authors sometimes communicate their messages through their characters, by showing how characters solve problems or deal with troubling events. Courage, friendship, and living with changes are themes authors often explore.

Activity: Suggest that students sketch a picture that communicates what they think is the message or theme of *Sidewalk Story*. Encourage them to share their sketches and talk about them.

VOCABULARY STRATEGIES

City Words

Discuss the setting of *Sidewalk Story* with students. Then have students go back into the text and find words that describe or relate to cities. For example, *reporter, photographer,* and *city desk* all have something to do with newspapers.

A possible word list:
- reporter
- photographer
- city desk

Literature Master 17
Use Prereading Strategies

Help students fill out the Reading Contract for *Sidewalk Story*. Students might preview the book in order to set a purpose for reading. Suggest that students look over the Activity Card and plan the activities they would like to do. Students should feel free to amend their contracts as necessary.
(*preview; set purpose*)

Literature Master 18
Build Language and Concepts

The prereading activity on Literature Master 18 helps students think about friends and how friends help each other. Students can share their responses to the friendship wheel if they feel comfortable doing so.
(*activate prior knowledge*)

Literature Master 19
Read Strategically

Literature Master 19 provides a graphic device for tracking events in the story and for deciding how exciting the events are. By connecting the dots, students show the rise and fall of the action in the story. Remind students that finished story graphs will differ. Encourage students to present their graphs and share their feelings about the story.
(*comprehension skill: draw conclusions*)

Literature Master 20
Share and Discuss

Encourage open response after students have read *Sidewalk Story*. Literature Master 20 provides questions to get book chat groups started. Or you might use the questions in your own conference with students. The Book Chat Guide provides space for students to write down their own questions or topics for discussion.
(*speaking and listening*)

EEk2 Comprehension Strategies (Bi) Set an appropriate purpose for reading and/or listening
NAPT Reading Comprehension Draw conclusions and make inferences

EEk2 Literary Appreciation (Diii) Use setting, characterization, story line, author's technique, and point of view to gain meaning
TAAS Reading Comprehension Perceive relationships and recognize outcomes in a variety of written texts (causes of a given event or a character's actions)

Assess / Wrap Up

■ CHECK ON THE READING ■

Conference with students after they finish reading *Sidewalk Story*. Suggest that they use their story graphs to remind them of what they have read. These questions might help you assess students' understanding of the story:

- What is the problem in the story? (*Do students explain that Lilly Etta's neighbors and best friend are being evicted from their apartment because of failure to pay rent?*)

- What events lead to a happy ending for Lilly Etta's friends? (*Do students explain that because of Lilly Etta's actions the case gets coverage from a TV station, and people offer help to the family?*)

- What kind of a friend is Lilly Etta? (*Do students use words such as determined, loyal, inventive, brave, and concerned?*)

(See also *Assessment Check* in the *BookFestival* assessment component.)

Activity Card 5
Respond (Side 1)

Activity Card 5 provides a prompt for students' personal response to *Sidewalk Story*. Students step into the story and explain who they would be and how they would help. Students can be creative in the details they add, but they should stay within the spirit and character of the story.
(critical and creative thinking)

The Activity Card suggests these ideas:

1. **Plan of Action** Students create a plan to help the family in the story.
   (use references)
2. **Character Diagram** Students draw the characters in the story and place themselves in their drawings.
   (visualize)
3. **Newspaper Article** Students write about story events as if they were newspaper reporters.
   (narrative writing)

EEk2 Study Strategies (Ciii) Locate information using the dictionary, encyclopedia, and other library references
EEk2 Literary Appreciation (Dii) Respond to various forms of literature representing the diversity of our literary heritage

Activity Card 5
Math Connection (Side 2)

Everyday money matters play a role in the events that occur in *Sidewalk Story*. On Activity Card 5 students are provided opportunities to explore the use of their math skills in solving everyday problems.
(make connections to personal life)

The Activity Card suggests these ideas:

1. **Do Lunch** Students compute the cost of lunch for the class.
   (solve problems)
2. **Spend a Million** Students use newspaper ads to find out what a million dollars will buy.
   (solve problems)
3. **Figure It Out** Students make up problems involving food or other items they use.
   (solve problems)

EEe1 Mathematics (F) Generate and extend problems
EEe4 Mathematics (G) Solve problems involving addition, subtraction, and multiplication of large numbers using calculators

ASSESS STUDENTS' ACTIVITIES

- **Respond:** Do students show an understanding of the Browns's predicament and suggest realistic ways to solve it?

- **Math Connection:** Do students use appropriate problem-solving skills?

- **Connect Home and School:** Invite students to check a telephone directory at home and talk to members of their family about members of their community who provide assistance to families. Students might write down what they find out and share it with the class.

Sidewalk Story

Tales of a Fourth Grade Nothing
by Judy Blume

• HIGHLIGHTS •

☑ average reading

Booktalk

This book will appeal to students who ...
* *read every Judy Blume book they can find,*
* *love humorous stories.*

Resources

◆ Activity Card 6

★ Literature Masters 21–24

★ Writing Master 6

Themes

Core Theme:
Caring

Related Themes:
Family Life
Wishes Come True
Pet Stories

Content

Literary Focus:
Characterization

Vocabulary Strategies:
Chat with a Character

Read Strategically:
Cause and Effect

Respond:
Help Wanted: Baby-sitter

Fine Arts Connection:
Make a Comic Book

MEETING INDIVIDUAL NEEDS

Choose As You Need

Students who are at risk might enjoy reading this book with a partner. 👫
Students with special needs might benefit from listening to a tape of the book prepared by another student. 💬 👤
Students who are achieving English proficiency might need a translation of Fudge's baby talk.
Students who enjoy challenges might prepare and read favorite chapters to their class or a younger class. 💬

Multicultural Connection

Community Culture

Many languages are spoken in New York City, where the Hatchers live. Students might enjoy translating some of the words from the book. How are the words *mother, brother, father, home, park, dog,* and *turtle* pronounced and written in Spanish, Korean, or Arabic, for example? Students can make and illustrate word cards showing translations in languages of their choice. ✏️

Activity Card 6
Respond (Side 1)

Activity Card 6 provides a prompt for students' personal response to *Tales of a Fourth Grade Nothing*. Students accept a baby-sitting job for Fudge and imagine what might happen. *(critical and creative thinking)*

The Activity Card suggests these ideas:

1. **Keep Notes** Students keep a baby-sitter's notebook and record advice Peter gives them about caring for Fudge.
(informative writing)

2. **Act It Out** Pairs of students act out a scene between Fudge and a baby-sitter.
(dramatize)

3. **Make a Poster** Students make a "Danger: Fudge" poster to warn other baby-sitters.
(informative writing)

 EEk1 Speaking (Biii) Entertain others with stories, poems, and dramatic activities
EEk2 Literary Appreciation (Diii) Use setting, characterization, story line, author's technique, and point of view to gain meaning

 Activity Card 6
Fine Arts Connection (Side 2)

Students can use their creativity as they design and write a comic book about Fudge. Remind students to keep Fudge true to character in his new adventures and to capture the humor that is in the book.
(narrative writing)

The Activity Card suggests these ideas:

1. **Cartoon Story** Students draw a cartoon strip for one of Fudge's new adventures.
(narrative writing)

2. **Letters to Peter** Students write a letter to Peter and also a response from him.
(persuasive writing)

3. **Cover Illustration** Students design and illustrate the cover for the first issue of the comic book series.
(visualize)

EEk3 Writing (Bv) Write in a variety of literary forms
EEe1 Fine Arts (Bi) Express individual ideas, thoughts, and feelings in simple media including drawing, painting, printmaking, constructing and modeling three-dimensional forms

ASSESS STUDENTS' ACTIVITIES

- **Respond:** Do students show that they understand the difficulties that Peter faces with a younger brother like Fudge?

- **Fine Arts Connection:** Do students' comic books reflect the humor of the book and the creativity of the students?

WRAP UP

- **Connect Home and School:** Invite students to ask their parents about something funny that they did when they were three. Students can share the incidents with the class. If possible, they can share photographs or videos of the incidents too.

Staying Nine
by Pam Conrad

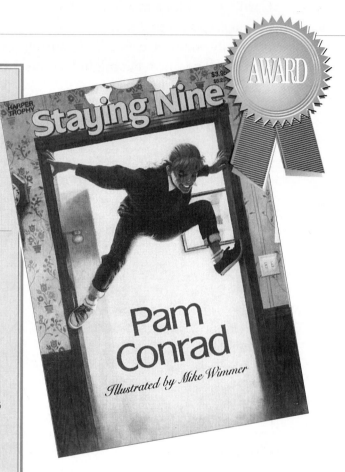

• HIGHLIGHTS •

☑ easy reading

Booktalk

This book will appeal to students who...
- *like to read about kids their own age,*
- *have ever thought about having an unbirthday party.*

Resources

◆ Activity Card 7

✪ Literature Masters 25–28

✪ Writing Master 7

Themes

Core Theme:

Family Customs

Related Themes:

Celebrations
Growing Up
Friends and Family

Content

Literary Focus:
Point of View

Vocabulary Strategies:
Descriptive Words

Read Strategically:
Sequence

Respond:
Describe Heather's Feelings

Science Connection:
Investigate Life Stages

MEETING INDIVIDUAL NEEDS

Choose As You Need

Students who are at risk might benefit from listening to a recording of the book made by another student.

Students with special needs might benefit from reading the selection with a partner.

Students who are achieving English proficiency might need some discussion on birthday traditions.

Students who enjoy challenges might read another book by Pam Conrad and compare it to *Staying Nine*.

Multicultural Connection

Ethnic Diversity

Students might enjoy finding out about birthday traditions in other countries around the world. How is a birthday celebrated? Are there special foods for the celebration? Are there certain birthdays that are significant? Students might compile their findings, illustrate them, and make a "Birthdays Around the World" display.

Summary

Heather Fitz likes being nine, and she refuses to turn ten! With the help of family and friends at her unbirthday party, she realizes that getting older isn't so bad after all.

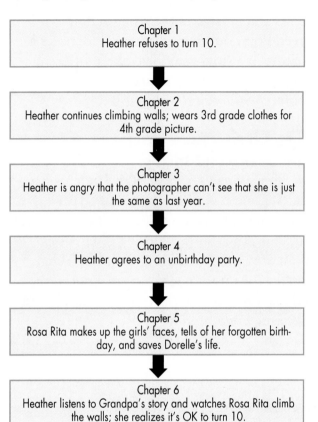

Chapter 1
Heather refuses to turn 10.

Chapter 2
Heather continues climbing walls; wears 3rd grade clothes for 4th grade picture.

Chapter 3
Heather is angry that the photographer can't see that she is just the same as last year.

Chapter 4
Heather agrees to an unbirthday party.

Chapter 5
Rosa Rita makes up the girls' faces, tells of her forgotten birthday, and saves Dorelle's life.

Chapter 6
Heather listens to Grandpa's story and watches Rosa Rita climb the walls; she realizes it's OK to turn 10.

The Author

When Pam Conrad was ten, she got sick with the chicken pox and had to stay in bed. Her mother gave her paper and crayons, thinking she would like to draw. But Pam wrote a poem instead and that was the start of her writing career. Conrad likes to write about almost anything: she has written picture books about bathtub toys, historical novels about people on the prairie, and books about everyday kids growing up in today's world.

More Books

Lexau, Joan M. *Striped Ice Cream.* (Lippincott, 1968). Becky wonders if the tradition of having chicken-spaghetti and striped ice cream will be upheld on her upcoming birthday.

De Angeli, Marguerite. *Thee, Hannah!* (Doubleday, 1940). A classic about a Quaker family's traditions in Pennsylvania.

Grifalconi, Ann. *The Village of Round and Square Houses.* (Little, Brown, 1986). Storytelling is the tradition in this African village, and a favorite involves a volcano!

LITERARY FOCUS

Point of View

Remind students that point of view is the author's choice of narrator, or the teller of the story. A writer can choose a character to tell a story, or a writer can choose a narrator who is outside of the story, as in *Staying Nine*. An outside narrator can tell what the characters say and do and sometimes what they think.

Activity: Students may want to try rewriting a favorite episode from *Staying Nine* from the point of view of one of the characters and discuss how that changes the story.

VOCABULARY STRATEGIES

Descriptive Words

Pam Conrad writes vivid descriptions of her characters in *Staying Nine*. She uses adjectives, adverbs, and strong verbs to make her writing vivid. Students can keep track of and classify these descriptive words and make flash cards to help learn them.

A possible list of vivid verbs:
- muttered
- shrugged
- scowled
- squinted

Staying Nine

Literature Master 25
Use Prereading Strategies

Help students fill out the Reading Contract for *Staying Nine*. Suggest that students preview illustrations and chapter titles. They should also preview the Activity Card to select activities for after reading. Point out that the contract is intended to help them plan their reading of *Staying Nine*. They should feel free to amend the dates on the contract as needed.
(*preview; set purpose*)

Literature Master 26
Build Language and Concepts

Students use a chart to organize what they like and dislike about their current age. Encourage students to add to their charts as they read *Staying Nine*. Students can share information on their charts if they wish. Do some students have the same dislikes and likes about their ages?
(*activate prior knowledge*)

EEk1 Speaking (Bv) Share information
EEk2 Comprehension Strategies (Bi) Set an appropriate purpose for reading and/or listening

Literature Master 27
Read Strategically

Staying Nine covers the week prior to Heather Fitz's tenth birthday. Literature Master 27 helps readers keep track of story events and illustrates the rising action in a novel. Point out that what one reader sees as exciting in a story may provoke a different reaction in a different reader.
(*comprehension skill: sequence*)

Literature Master 28
Share and Discuss

Encourage open response after students have read *Staying Nine*. This page can be used to jot down students' questions and comments. Students can refer to it during discussions about *Staying Nine* during their book chat. You may want to model a sample question and response during their book chat.
(*speaking and listening*)

EEk2 Comprehension Strategies (Bii) Develop literal meaning through recognition of details and sequential order
TAAS Reading Comprehension Identify supporting ideas in a variety of written texts (Sequence)

Assess / Wrap Up

■ CHECK ON THE READING ■

Talk with students after they finish reading *Staying Nine*. Have them use their story graphs to remind them of events in the story. These questions might help you assess students' understanding of the story:

- What effect does her approaching birthday have on Heather Fitz? *(Do students recognize Heather's fear of change?)*

- If Heather were your friend, what advice would you have given her about her tenth birthday? *(Can students relate to Heather's fear? Can they put themselves in her situation?)*

- How does Heather's birthday celebration compare with yours? Describe similarities and differences. *(Can students verbalize their birthday traditions and compare them to Heather's?)*

(See also *Assessment Check* in the *BookFestival* assessment component.)

Activity Card 7
Respond (Side 1)

Activity Card 7 provides a prompt for students' personal response to *Staying Nine*. Students reflect on Heather Fitz's dilemma in *Staying Nine* and decide if they agree with her or not.

(critical and creative thinking)

The Activity Card suggests these ideas:

1. **Take a Poll** Students survey classmates on their feelings about Heather's refusal to turn ten and present their findings in graph form.
   (graphs)
2. **Write a Letter** Students pretend to be a character and write to Heather convincing her to have her birthday. ◄▬▬ED
   (persuasive writing)
3. **Make a List** Students list what they think Heather fears about turning ten. ◄▬▬ED
   (make inferences)

 EEk2 Comprehension Strategies (Biv) Develop inferential meaning
EEk3 Writing (Draft) (Bvi) Write using a variety of correspondence formats

Activity Card 7
Science Connection (Side 2)

Students can explore the advantages and disadvantages of different ages as they work to create a Life Stages Booklet. Remind students to use reference sources for factual information and to interview people for anecdotal information.

(use references sources; conduct interviews)

The Activity Card suggests these ideas:

1. **Definitions** Students define life stages and list advantages and disadvantages of each. ◄▬▬ED
   (informative writing)
2. **Personal Reactions** Students write interview questions on a life stage, interview a family member, and write a summary of the interview. ◄▬▬ED
   (informative writing)
3. **Illustrations** Students illustrate their Life Stages Booklet with photographs, drawings, or magazine cutouts.
   (art activity)

EEk1 Listening (Aii) Listen to receive direction, gain information, and enhance appreciation of language
EEe4 Science (A) Obtain science information from varied resources

---

ASSESS STUDENTS' ACTIVITIES

WRAP UP

- **Respond:** Do students show that they understand Heather's reluctance to turn ten? 📖

- **Science Connection:** Do students' Life Stages Booklets accurately describe the various life stages? Is the factual information complemented with personal anecdotes and illustrations? 📖

- **Connect Home and School:** Invite students to interview a family member about either their least favorite or most favorite birthday. Students can share their interview findings orally during a class discussion or in a paragraph summarizing the interview. 💬 ◄▬▬ED

Staying Nine

Willie Mays: Young Superstar
by Louis Sabin

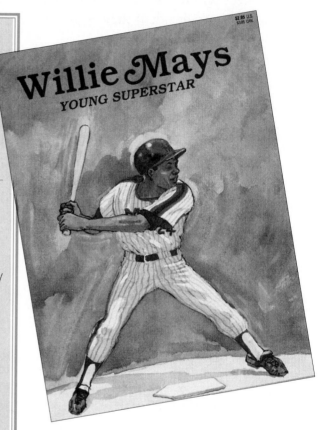

Willie Mays
YOUNG SUPERSTAR

• HIGHLIGHTS •

☑ average reading

Booktalk

This book will appeal to students who ...
- *like to read books about real people,*
- *enjoy learning about sports heroes.*

Resources

◆ Activity Card 8

✪ Literature Masters 29–32

✪ Writing Master 8

Themes

Core Theme:
Family Support

Related Themes:
Dreamers and Achievers
Let's Find Out

Content

Literary Focus:
Narrative Nonfiction

Vocabulary Strategies:
Compile a Baseball Dictionary

Read Strategically:
Sequence

Respond:
Join Willie's Team

Language Arts Connection:
Our Superstars

MEETING INDIVIDUAL NEEDS

Students who are at risk might enjoy comparing Willie Mays's baseball statistics with those of current baseball stars.

Students with special needs might like to listen to a student-made audiotape of the book. 💬

Students who are achieving English proficiency might benefit from discussing what they already know about baseball and great baseball players. 💬 🗣

Students who enjoy challenges might enjoy looking up old newspaper articles about Willie Mays and sharing them with the class.

Multicultural Connection

Values

Students might enjoy discussing the values that Willie Mays learned from his family. What was important to Willie Mays's father and his family? What values did Willie Mays learn from them? How did those values influence him as a person? Students could work alone or with a partner to make a list of the values they think are most important in a family, and then discuss their lists in small groups. Encourage an atmosphere of respect for everyone's opinions. 👪

Summary

At an age when many children are barely crawling, six-month-old Willie Mays already enjoyed chasing a ball. Thanks to his father's unflagging support as well as his own outstanding abilities, Mays later went on to a twenty-three year career as a Major League baseball superstar.

1979	Elected to Baseball Hall of Fame
1973	Helps the Mets win the National League pennant; retires from baseball
1972	Joins the New York Mets
1954	Wins the National League batting title
1951	Helps the Giants win the pennant
1950	Signed by the New York Giants
1948–1949	Plays for the Black Barons in the Negro Leagues
1945–1946	Plays in the Industrial League with his father
1944	At 13, joins the semiprofessional Gray Sox
1941	At 10, his family moves into their "dream house"
1936	At 5, starts to play catch with his dad
1931	Born in Westfield, Alabama

The Author

Louis Sabin is a prolific author who has also written books under the pen names of Keith Brandt, Larry Bains, and Louis Santry. He worked as an editor before becoming a writer, and his first publishing credits were for crossword puzzles. The author of dozens of books, Louis Sabin enjoys sports, popular and classical music, and reading.

More Books

Sabin, Louis. *Thomas Alva Edison: Young Inventor.* (Troll Associates, 1983). This inspiring biography tells how an inquisitive child grew up to be a world famous inventor.

Slote, Alfred. *The Trading Game.* (Lippincott, 1990). Andy doesn't know why his mother does not want his grandfather, a former Major League player, to coach Andy's baseball team. When Andy realizes why, he gains new insight into himself, his deceased father, and his grandfather.

LITERARY FOCUS

Narrative Nonfiction

Remind students that in narrative nonfiction, an author uses factual information to tell a true story about a person or event. Biography and autobiography are both narrative nonfiction.

Activity: As students read, ask them to notice how the information about Willie Mays is organized. In what order does the author tell about events in Willie Mays's life? Students can keep notes while they read and share their observations in a discussion.

VOCABULARY STRATEGIES

Compile a Baseball Dictionary

Willie Mays: Young Superstar is loaded with baseball terms that may not be familiar to students. Students can compile an illustrated baseball dictionary with words and phrases such as *catcher's mask, dugout, rookie,* and *shortstop.*

A possible word list:
- catcher's mask
- dugout
- rookie
- shortstop

Willie Mays: Young Superstar

Literature Master 29
Use Prereading Strategies

Help students fill out the Reading Contract for *Willie Mays: Young Superstar*. Suggest students preview the book by looking through the illustrations. Students may also skim Activity Card 8 to select activities to complete after reading. Students may adjust their contracts later as needed.

(preview; set purpose)

Literature Master 30
Build Language and Concepts

Before reading, students may find it helpful to review what they know about baseball. Literature Master 30 invites students to fill in the playing positions around a baseball diamond, and to discuss how the game is played.

(activate prior knowledge)

Literature Master 31
Read Strategically

Willie Mays: Young Superstar describes Willie Mays's achievements over a lifetime. Literature Master 31 helps students keep track of the most important events by providing a time line that can be filled in as they read.

(comprehension skill: sequence)

Literature Master 32
Share and Discuss

Encourage open response from students when they discuss *Willie Mays: Young Superstar*. Literature Master 32 suggests some questions for discussion during a book chat or a conference. Students can add their own questions and comments about the book.

(speaking and listening)

EEk2 Vocabulary (Aiv) Acquire a reading vocabulary relating to concepts being learned
EEk2 Comprehension Strategies (Bi) Set an appropriate purpose for reading and/or listening

EEk2 Comprehension Strategies (Bii) Develop literal meaning through recognition of details and sequential order
NAPT Reading Comprehension Recognize stated factual information

Assess / Wrap Up

■ CHECK ON THE READING ■

Conference with students after they finish reading *Willie Mays: Young Superstar*. Their time lines may help them recall the main events in the book. These questions might help you assess students' understanding:

- How did Willie Mays's family influence the kind of person he became? *(Do students discuss the strong support and positive example that Mays's family provided?)*

- How did Willie Mays prepare for a career in baseball? *(Do students recognize that Mays worked hard from childhood on to perfect his playing abilities?)*

- What do you think people will remember about Willie Mays? *(Are students able to sum up his athletic achievements? Do they mention his winning personality?)*

(See also Assessment Check in the BookFestival assessment component.)

Activity Card 8
Respond (Side 1)

Students step back in time to Willie Mays's childhood and join his neighborhood baseball team. The activities invite them to describe what they like best about being friends with young Willie Mays.
(critical and creative thinking)

The Activity Card suggests these ideas:
1. **Write a Letter** Students write to Willie Mays to plan an afternoon together.
   (expressive writing)
2. **Create a Skit** Students make up a skit about spending the day with Willie Mays.
   (dramatize)
3. **Compose Yourself** Students compose a song, story, poem, or rap about Willie Mays and perform it for the class.
   (entertain)

 EEk1 Speaking (Biii) Entertain others with stories, poems, and dramatic activities
EEk2 Literary Appreciation (Dv) Participate in cooperative learning and a variety of oral activities to elicit meaning

Activity Card 8
Language Arts Connection (Side 2)

Students take a cue from baseball card collectors and make a collection of cards featuring the members of their class.
(synthesize information)

The Activity Card suggests these ideas:
1. **Interviews** Students gather information for the cards by interviewing classmates.
   (conduct interviews)
2. **Contributions** Students write sentences to describe each class member's contributions.
   (informative writing)
3. **Portraits** Students collect their classmates' photos or drawn portraits for the front of each card.
   (use graphic sources)

EEk1 Listening (Aii) Listen to receive direction, gain information, and enhance appreciation of language
EEk3 Writing (Draft) (Bv) Write in a variety of literary forms

ASSESS STUDENTS' ACTIVITIES

- **Respond:** Do students show that they have a sense of the kind of friend Willie Mays would be?

- **Language Arts Connection:** Do students' card collections highlight the unique qualities and special contributions of their classmates?

WRAP UP

- **Connect Home and School:** Students can poll friends and family members to find out if any of them are baseball fans. If so, what do they know about Willie Mays? Can they share any stories about his career? Students can report the information they receive to the class.

Esio Trot
by Roald Dahl

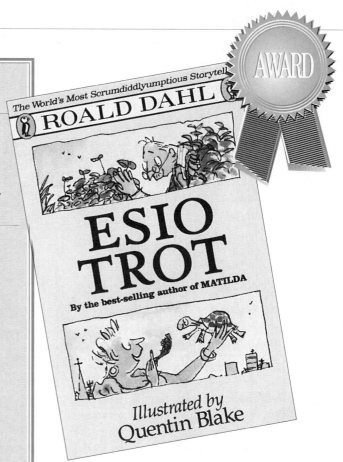

· HIGHLIGHTS ·

☑ easy reading

Booktalk

This book will appeal to students who ...
- *enjoy books by Roald Dahl,*
- *like books with happily-ever-after endings.*

Resources

◆ Activity Card 9

✪ Literature Masters 33–36

✪ Writing Master 9

Themes

Core Theme:

Animals Matter

Related Themes:

Pet Stories
Problem Solving
Wishes Come True

Content

Literary Focus:
Dialogue

Vocabulary Strategies:
Translating to Tortoise

Read Strategically:
Summarize

Respond:
Be Part of the Story

Math Connection:
Learn About Pets

Choose As You Need

MEETING INDIVIDUAL NEEDS

Students who are at risk might listen to a tape of the book prepared by another student. 〝👤

Students with special needs might read the book with a partner. 👬

Students who are achieving English proficiency might need extra help with the vocabulary.

Students who enjoy challenges might make an audiotape of the book for other students to use. 💬

Multicultural Connection

Community Culture

Students might enjoy learning about traditional English tea time. When is tea time? What foods are served? How do the British take their tea? Perhaps the class could have a tea time. To extend the study, students might compare British tea traditions to Japanese tea traditions. 👥👥

Summary

Shy Mr. Hoppy loves his widowed neighbor Mrs. Silver from afar. His ingenious plan to help Mrs. Silver's tortoise Alfie grow bigger also helps Mr. Hoppy win Mrs. Silver's heart.

The Problem

Mr. Hoppy is too shy to tell Mrs. Silver how he feels about her.

The Action

He tries to impress her by devising a plan to help her make her tortoise Alfie grow.

The Result

Mr. Hoppy's plan works, Mrs. Silver falls in love with him, and they live happily ever after. So does Alfie!

The Author

Roald (pronounced Roo-aal) Dahl never considered writing as a career until he was about twenty-four and wrote an article about his most memorable war experience for a magazine. He mostly wrote for adults until his children were born. The stories he told them at bedtime made him aware of the kinds of stories that hold children's interest. *James and the Giant Peach* and *Charlie and the Chocolate Factory* are among his most famous children's books.

More Books

DeJong, Meindert. *Along Came a Dog.* (Harper, 1958). In this award-winning story, a big black dog longs to become part of a barnyard family, but all he finds at first is a little red hen and much trouble.

Damjan, Mischa. *Atuk.* (North-South Books, 1990). Atuk loves his little brown sled dog, Taruk. He dreams that someday they will lead their own team. When Taruk is attacked by a wolf, Atuk learns to turn his hate for the wolf into love.

LITERARY FOCUS

Dialogue

Remind students that dialogue is conversation between characters. Dialogue can be used to reveal character, provide background, and move the plot forward. Review how dialogue is written—the speakers' words are enclosed in quotation marks, a dialogue tag such as "she said" identifies the speaker, and a new paragraph begins each time the speaker changes.

Activity: As students read *Esio Trot*, have them select a favorite section of dialogue to prepare and read to the class with a partner.

VOCABULARY STRATEGIES

Translating to Tortoise

Students learn tortoise talk from Mr. Hoppy. They can keep track of words that they might want to use to write to Alfie. They might want to ask about a tortoise's diet and write the words *tomato, lettuce,* and *celery* in "tortoise" as well as English.

A possible word list:
- tomato, otamot
- lettuce, ecuttel
- celery, yrelec

Esio Trot

Literature Master 33
Use Prereading Strategies

Help students fill out the Reading Contract for *Esio Trot*. Suggest that students preview the book cover and illustrations. Students should also read the Activity Card to select activities for after reading. Students should feel free to amend the contract as needed.
(preview; set purpose)

Literature Master 34
Build Language and Concepts

Groups of students might use their charts to discuss strategies for making friends.

Literature Master 35
Read Strategically

Esio Trot shows how Mr. Hoppy solves a problem. Literature Master 35 helps students analyze Mr. Hoppy's problem and summarize the plot of the book.
(comprehension skill: summarize)

Literature Master 36
Share and Discuss

Encourage open response after students have read groups of pages from *Esio Trot*, or after they have completed the book. The Book Chat Guide can be used by students to jot down predictions, questions, and comments about the characters and plot of *Esio Trot*. You might want to use the questions during your own conference with students as well.
(speaking and listening)

EEk2 Comprehension Strategies (Bi) Set an appropriate purpose for reading and/or listening
TAAS Reading Comprehension Analyze information in a variety of written texts (Understand the feelings and emotions of characters)

EEk2 Comprehension Strategies (Bii) Develop literal meaning through recognition of details and sequential order
NAPT Reading Comprehension Infer the traits, feelings, and motivations of characters

Assess / Wrap Up

■ CHECK ON THE READING ■

Conference with students after they finish reading *Esio Trot*. Suggest that they review Literature Masters 35 and 36. These questions might help you assess students' understanding of the story:

• What do you think of Mr. Hoppy's plan? *(Do students realize that the plan is deceptive, even though it works?)*

• What do you think of Mrs. Silver? *(Do students think she is really dense, or do they think she is using Alfie to get to know Mr. Hoppy? Do they support their opinions?)*

• Is this story realistic? Why or why not? *(Are students able to express and support an opinion?)*

(See also Assessment Check in the BookFestival assessment component.)

Activity Card 9
Respond (Side 1)

Activity Card 9 provides a prompt for students' personal response to *Esio Trot*. Students walk (or crawl!) into the story and become one of the characters. They express how they feel about the events in the story. *(critical and creative thinking)*

The Activity Card suggests these ideas:
1. **Talk Turtle** Students perform a skit in which they are the turtles in Mr. Hoppy's apartment discussing recent events. ♦♦♦♦
(dramatize)
2. **Write a Letter** Students write a letter from one of the character's points of view explaining recent events.
(informative writing)
3. **Make a Model** Students draw or make a model to demonstrate Mr. Hoppy's plan.
(visualize)

EEk1 Speaking (Biii) Entertain others with stories, poems, and dramatic activities
EEk2 Literary Appreciation (Diii) Use setting, characterization, story line, author's technique, and point of view to gain meaning

 ## Activity Card 9
Math Connection (Side 2)

Students can explore the kinds of pets that members of the class have and research facts about those pets.
(use reference sources)

The Activity Card suggests these ideas:
1. **Popular Pets** Students survey classmates about pets and graph the results according to popularity of pets.
(use graphic sources)
2. **Pet Report** Students write a report about a particular pet.
(informative writing).
3. **Feeding Your Pet** Students research the cost of feeding four different types of pets and chart the results.
(use graphic sources)

EEk2 Study Strategies (Civ) Interpret graphic sources in meaningful context
EEe7 Mathematics (A) Collect, record, and organize data into tables, charts, bar graphs, and line graphs

ASSESS STUDENTS' ACTIVITIES

- **Respond:** Do students show that they understand the characters and their feelings?

- **Math Connection:** Do students' pet projects show students' ability to gather information and organize it? Are the graphic aids easy to understand?

WRAP UP

- **Connect Home and School:** Invite students to write messages about *Esio Trot* to their families in tortoise talk. Can they decode it? If so, they should write brief replies. In tortoise, of course! Alternatively, they can reply with a coded message for students to decipher.

Esio Trot

Sarah, Plain and Tall
by Patricia MacLachlan

HIGHLIGHTS

☑ easy reading

Booktalk
This book will appeal to students who ...
- *enjoy early American realistic stories,*
- *need information about pioneer life.*

Resources
◆ Activity Card 10
✪ Literature Masters 37–40
✪ Writing Master 10

Themes
Core Theme:
Places of the Past
Related Themes:
Pioneers
Life on a Farm
All Kinds of Families

Content
Literary Focus:
Historical Fiction
Vocabulary Strategies:
Illustrating Prairie Life
Read Strategically:
Compare and Contrast
Respond:
Journey Back in Time
Social Studies Connection:
Be a Reporter

Choose As You Need

MEETING INDIVIDUAL NEEDS

Students who are at risk might enjoy reading the story with a partner. 👬
Students with special needs might enjoy listening to the story on a tape, either one made by other students or a version by actress Glenn Close. 🔊👤
Students who are achieving English proficiency might benefit from discussing what it was like living on a farm during pioneer times. 💬 🔊👤
Students who enjoy challenges might want to prepare an audiotape of the story for their peers. 💬

Multicultural Connection

Community Culture
The way of life is quite different between Sarah's home in Maine and her new home on the Midwest prairie. Students might enjoy finding out about ways of life in different parts of the country. How does geographic location affect and determine what foods people eat, what clothes they wear, and their modes of transportation throughout the year? Students might present their findings on illustrated maps.

Summary

Anna and Caleb's father invites a mail-order bride to come to live with them in their prairie home. The children are captivated by Sarah and hope she'll stay.

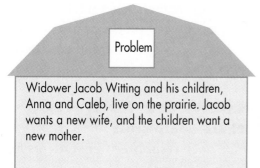

Problem

Widower Jacob Witting and his children, Anna and Caleb, live on the prairie. Jacob wants a new wife, and the children want a new mother.

Solution

Jacob advertises for a wife in a Maine newspaper. Sarah Wheaton answers the ad and comes to visit on a trial basis for a month.

Over time, strong and independent Sarah becomes attached to the children and Jacob, and they too are enraptured by her.

The Author

When award-winning author Patricia MacLachlan was asked to write a script for a two-hour tele-vised screenplay of *Sarah, Plain and Tall*, she had to write in a way she had never done before. To write the script, she had to add and develop additional characters and substantially rewrite the story. When Ms. MacLachlan wants to develop a new story, she first thinks about and becomes thor-oughly acquainted with her characters. Once she is comfort-able with them, the plot seems to natural-ly fall into place.

More Books

MacLachlan, Patricia. *Through Grandpa's Eyes.* (Harper, 1980). John and his blind grandfather have a wonderful, close rela-tionship. Grandpa shares with John the special way he "sees" and gets around in the world.

Wilder, Laura Ingalls. *Farmer Boy.* (Harper, 1933). Laura Ingalls grew up and married Almanzo Wilder. However, about one hundred years ago, Almanzo was nine and living on a farm in New York. *Farmer Boy* tells the story of one year in the life of the Wilders on their farm.

LITERARY FOCUS

Historical Fiction

Remind students that historical fiction is set in the past, and time and place determine the setting. In historical fiction all details, such as clothing, food, and activities, must fit the story's time and place. Characters may be real or invented.

Activity: As students read the book, suggest they use a chart to compare aspects of Sarah's life in the 1800s with their own. They might enjoy using the details from their charts to write other episodes in the life of a child during the 1800s.

VOCABULARY STRATEGIES

Illustrating Prairie Life

Sarah, Plain and Tall describes many aspects of life on a prairie farm. Students can keep track of these related words and phrases and use them to create illustrated booklets for each other. For example, *prairie violets, rolling land,* and *windmill* describe the prairie setting.

A possible word list describing prairie life:
- prairie violets
- rolling land
- windmill

Literature Master 37
Use Prereading Strategies

Help students fill out the Reading Contract for *Sarah, Plain and Tall*. They might skim the Activity Card to preview activities for after reading. Students should feel free to amend the contract as needed.
(preview; set purpose)

Literature Master 38
Build Language and Concepts

Students are to create an advertisement that would encourage someone to move to their town. They are to describe the town and tell what is pleasing and exciting about living there. Groups of students might enjoy working together on this activity
(activate prior knowledge)

Literature Master 39
Read Strategically

As students read *Sarah, Plain and Tall*, they will find that there are many indications that Sarah might return to Maine. Literature Master 39 helps readers keep track of the reasons Sarah has to stay on the prairie and the reasons she has to return to Maine.
(comprehension skill: compare and contrast)

Literature Master 40
Share and Discuss

Encourage open response after students have read groups of chapters or have completed the book. Literature Master 40 provides starter questions for literature groups. Students can also use this page to jot down questions or comments they wish to discuss. You might use the questions during your own conference with students as well.
(speaking and listening)

EEk2 Comprehension Strategies (Bi) Set an appropriate purpose for reading and/or listening
TAAS Reading Comprehension Identify supporting details in a variety of written texts (describe setting)

EEk1 Listening (Ai) Focus attention on and listen to both adult and peer speakers during large and small group interactions
NAPT Reading Comprehension Infer the traits, feelings, and motivations of characters

Assess / Wrap Up

■ CHECK ON THE READING ■

Conference with students after they complete *Sarah, Plain and Tall*. Suggest that they use their comparison charts to remind them of the events in the story. These questions might help you assess students' understanding of the story:

• How do the different clues that Sarah might return to Maine affect Caleb and Anna? *(Do students express the uncertain feelings of Caleb and Anna?)*

• If you had lived on the Witting farm, what would have been your favorite chore? What would you have done in your free time? *(Do students demonstrate an understanding of prairie farm life?)*

• How are Caleb and Anna's lives different from yours? How are their lives similar to yours? Describe these similarities and differences. *(Are students able to verbalize how historical periods affect the lives of individuals?)*

(See also Assessment Check in the BookFestival assessment component.)

Activity Card 10
Respond (Side 1)

Activity Card 10 prompts students' personal response to the book. Students journey back to the Witting farm in time machines to become part of *Sarah, Plain and Tall*. Remind students to use the details from the scene, but to go beyond what the author has created to include themselves.
(critical and creative thinking)

The Activity Card suggests these ideas:
1. **Write a Letter** Students write a letter home explaining one day on the Witting farm.
   (descriptive writing)
2. **Act It Out** Partners plan and perform a script for the scene they choose.
   (dramatize)
3. **Make a Scene** Students illustrate the scene as they see it in their mind.
   (visualize)

 EEk1 Speaking (Biii) Entertain others with stories, poems, and dramatic activities
EEk2 Literary Appreciation (Diii) Use setting, characterization, story line, author's technique, and point of view to gain meaning

 Activity Card 10
Social Studies Connection (Side 2)

Students can explore various aspects of pioneer life while researching parts of a newspaper. Students assume the roles of pioneer newspaper editors. Remind them to report on what pioneers might think is important or interesting reading.
(use reference sources)

The Activity Card suggests these ideas:
1. **Current Events** Students write about an event that took place at about the time of *Sarah, Plain and Tall*.
   (informative writing)
2. **Recipes or Instructions** Students write recipes or instructions for pioneer foods or farm activities.
   (informative writing)
3. **Advertisements** Students create ads appropriate to the time of *Sarah, Plain and Tall*.
   (persuasive writing)

EEk2 Study Strategies (Ciii) Locate information using the dictionary, encyclopedia, and other library references including data base searching strategies
EEe5 Social Studies (B) Understand how people adapt to their physical environment

ASSESS STUDENTS' ACTIVITIES

- **Respond:** Do students show that they understand what is happening in the scene they chose?

- **Social Studies Connection:** Do students' newspapers demonstrate an appreciation of what was important to pioneers?

WRAP UP

- **Connect Home and School:** Invite students to interview parents, grandparents, and if possible, great-grandparents to find out about differences in their lives as they were growing up. How were their childhood years different from today's children?

Sarah, Plain and Tall

Grandma Moses: Painter of Rural America
by Zibby Oneal

• HIGHLIGHTS •

☑ challenging reading

Booktalk

This book will appeal to students who ...
- *enjoy reading biographies,*
- *are interested in famous artists.*

Resources

◆ Activity Card 11

★ Literature Masters 41–44

★ Writing Master 11

Themes

Core Theme:

Ways of Seeing

Related Themes:

Nature
Imagination
Times Past

Content

Literary Focus:
Biography

Vocabulary Strategies:
Artist's Materials

Read Strategically:
Details and Facts

Respond:
Step into Grandma's Life

Social Studies Connection:
Past, Present, Future

Choose As You Need

MEETING INDIVIDUAL NEEDS

Students who are at risk might enjoy reading the book with a partner. 👬

Students with special needs might benefit from listening to the book on an audiotape made by another student. 🗣💬

Students who are achieving English proficiency might want to discuss the paintings reproduced in the book before they read.

Students who enjoy challenges might want to prepare an exhibit of biographies and autobiographies of or by different artists.

Multicultural Connection

Ethnic Diversity

Students might enjoy finding books, reproductions, posters, and photographs of works of art that are traditional in style to different ethnic groups. What materials are used to create the art? What cultural traditions are represented in the art? Students might discuss the similarities and differences among the works of art. 💬🗣

Summary

This biography, Grandma Moses: Painter of Rural America, *covers the interesting and varied life of Anna Mary Robertson, better known as Grandma Moses, from her birth in 1860 to her death in 1961.*

> Grandma Moses: Born Anna Mary Robertson on a farm in New York in 1860.

> As a hard-working farm wife and mother, she raised a large family and started her own butter business. The profits allowed her family to purchase a dairy farm. Later she successfully made and sold potato chips, a relatively uncommon food product at the time.

> Her most successful career was as a self-taught artist. She began this famous phase of her life when she was in her seventies and continued until her death in 1961.

The Author

Before Zibby Oneal wrote *Grandma Moses: Painter of Rural America*, she studied Grandma Moses's paintings and read articles about her, as well as her autobiography, *My Life's History*. Ms. Oneal, an art lover, has said that if she were not a writer, she would like to be a painter. Ms. Oneal's interest in art is also reflected in her novels. Some of the characters in her novels are painters.

More Books

Raboff, Ernest. *Marc Chagall.* (HarperCollins Children's Books, 1988). Chagall's bright imaginative paintings of everyday lives are explained. Behind each picture is a story of happiness or love.

Stren, Patti. *There's a Rainbow in My Closet.* (Harper, 1979). No one understands Emma's art. She paints what she feels and draws what's real. But what's real to her isn't at all real to her teacher. Emma is caught between pleasing her teacher and creating her dreams.

LITERARY FOCUS

Biography

Remind students that a biography is an account of a person's life written by another person. It may cover a person's whole life, only a part of it, or a single incident.

Activity: As students read *Grandma Moses: Painter of Rural America*, suggest that they make a time line to keep track of the events they find most interesting. They might enjoy comparing what they think was most interesting with other students who have read the book.

VOCABULARY STRATEGIES

Artist's Materials

Grandma Moses talks about different materials the artist used to create her artwork. Students can keep track of these materials and use them to play a "Twenty Questions" type of game with each other. Some materials are *crushed berries*, a *windowpane*, and *match sticks*.

A possible list of artist's materials:
- crushed berries
- windowpane
- match sticks

Literature Master 41
Use Prereading Strategies

Help students fill out the Reading Contract for *Grandma Moses: Painter of Rural America*. Suggest that students read the chapter titles and preview the artwork. They might also skim the Activity Card to preview the activities for after reading. They should feel free to amend the contract as needed.
(preview; set purpose)

 ## Literature Master 42
Build Language and Concepts

Groups of students might compare what they know about artists and how they work. After reading, students might want to add more facts to the picture frames.
(activate prior knowledge)

 ## Literature Master 43
Read Strategically

Grandma Moses: Painter of Rural America is about the long life of Grandma Moses. Literature Master 43 will help students keep track of the facts and details about her life as they read.
(comprehension skill: details and facts)

 ## Literature Master 44
Share and Discuss

Encourage open response after students have read each group of chapters in *Grandma Moses*, and again after they have finished the book. This Book Chat Guide provides questions to get students talking about the book. Students can also use this page to jot down questions or comments they wish to discuss. You might want to use the questions during your own conference with students as well.

(speaking and listening)

EEk2 Comprehension Strategies (Bi) Set an appropriate purpose for reading and/or listening
TAAS Reading Comprehension Identify supporting details in a variety of written texts (facts and details)

EEk1 Speaking (Bv) Share information
NAPT Reading Comprehension Recognize stated factual information

■ CHECK ON THE READING ■

Conference with students after they finish reading *Grandma Moses*. Suggest that they use their details web to remind them of events in the story. These questions might help you assess students' understanding of the book:

- What early childhood events influenced Anna Mary Robertson to become a painter later in her life? *(Do students indicate an understanding of the events that influenced her?)*

- What was Grandma Moses's attitude about all the recognition she received because of her artwork? *(Do students demonstrate an understanding of Grandma Moses's astonishment and discomfort with all the attention she received?)*

- Explain how Grandma Moses's childhood in the 1860s differs from your own. How was it the same as yours? *(Are students able to verbalize the similarities and differences between their childhood and that of Grandma Moses?)*

(See also Assessment Check in the BookFestival assessment component.)

After Reading

Activity Card 11
Respond (Side 1)

The Activity Card provides a choice of activities for students' personal responses to *Grandma Moses*. Students step into scenes from Grandma Moses's life and describe what happens.
(critical and creative thinking)

The Activity Card suggests these ideas:
1. **Make a Scene** Students draw or paint a scene from Grandma Moses's life.
   (visualize)
2. **Send a Letter** Students become Grandma Moses and write a letter to one of her children that describes her newest paintings. ◄██▆D
   (descriptive writing)
3. **Write a Poem** Students write a poem about one of Grandma Moses's paintings. ◄██▆D
   (expressive writing)

 EEk3 Writing (Bv) Write in a variety of literary forms
EEk3 Writing (Bvi) Write using a variety of correspondence formats

Activity Card 11
Social Studies Connection (Side 2)

Students can explore ways of life from the past, present, and future. They can examine old photographs or magazines to learn about the past, observe things around them to notice the present, and look in science magazines to discover the future.
(synthesize information)

The Activity Card suggests these ideas:
1. **Everyday Scenes** Students draw or paint a detailed scene from their own lives.
   (visualize)
2. **Interview Time** Students interview adults about childhood memories, write them down, and share them with the class. ◄██▆D
   (informative writing)
3. **Skit from the Future** Students put on a skit showing a typical day in the future. ♦♦♦♦
   (work cooperatively to enhance meaning)

EEe1 Fine Arts (Bi) Express individual ideas, thoughts, and feelings in simple media
EEe5 Social Studies (B) Understand how people adapt to their physical environment

---

ASSESS STUDENTS' ACTIVITIES

- **Respond:** In their chosen scene do they show an understanding of Grandma Moses's varied and interesting life? Do they describe her paintings in their letters? Do their poems express what they see and feel in Grandma Moses's painting? 📖

- **Social Studies Connection:** Do students' demonstrate an understanding about how life changes through the years? Do they recognize some of the factors that change ways of life? 📖

WRAP UP

- **Connect Home and School:** Invite students to take *Grandma Moses* home to share with their families. Students can poll family members about which of Grandma Moses's paintings they liked best. What are their reasons for their choice? Students can share the results of their poll with the class.

Grandma Moses

Kickle Snifters and Other Fearsome Critters
collected by Alvin Schwartz

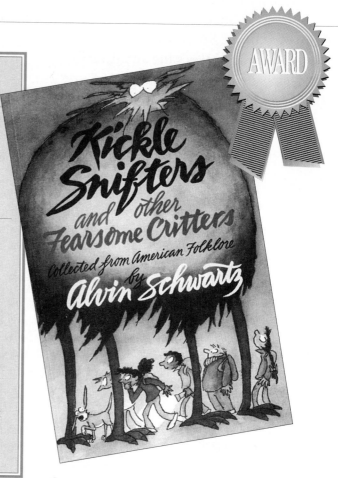

HIGHLIGHTS

☑ easy reading

Booktalk

This book will appeal to students who ...
- *have active imaginations,*
- *enjoy folklore,*
- *appreciate humorous illustrations.*

Resources

◆ Activity Card 12

✪ Literature Masters 45–48

✪ Writing Master 12

Themes

Core Theme:
Creativity

Related Themes:
Imagination
Tall Tales
Animal Stories

Content

Literary Focus:
Figurative Language

Vocabulary Strategies:
Define the Critters

Read Strategically:
Classify

Respond:
Favorite Critters

Language Arts Connection:
Create a Zoo

Choose as You Need

MEETING INDIVIDUAL NEEDS

Students who are at risk might work in small groups, divide up the chapters, prepare, and read them aloud to each other. 🛉🛉🛉

Students with special needs might read the book with a partner. 🛉🛉

Students who are achieving English proficiency might need assistance with the names of the imaginary creatures.

Students who enjoy challenges might prepare and read the poem "The Raggedy Man" by James Whitcomb Riley to the class. 🗨

Multicultural Connection

Community Culture

Students might enjoy finding out about creatures that can be found in the folklore of other countries. For example, leprechauns and banshees are creatures famous in the folklore of Ireland. Students can make drawings of their creatures, write a brief description of each, and compile them in a book for the class to share. ◄▬▬▌

Summary

American folklore is populated with amazing imaginary creatures. Meet some of them in Kickle Snifters and Other Fearsome Critters.

Fearsome Critters

Most Likely to Wake the Baby	
squonk	gowrow
windigo	glyptodont
tree-squeak	

Useful on a Camping Trip
milamo bird
billdad
slide-rock bolter
hoopajuba

You'd Like to Meet	
snawfus	joint snake
goofus bird	whing-whang
side-hill gouger	wunk
squidgicum-squee	

You'd Run Away From Fast	
hugag	lufferlang
splinter cat	tripodero
timberdoodle	jump-at-a-body
hide-behind	hoop snake

Most Likely to Cheer You If You're Feeling Sad
rubberado
sea serpent
kickle snifter

The Author

Alvin Schwartz's first piece of writing was a newspaper filled with gossip and news about his family, which included dozens of aunts, uncles, and cousins who lived within a mile or two of him. He had only one copy (typewritten at that time), so he rented it by the day to anyone who wanted to read it. A quick glance at a card catalog today will show that Alvin Schwartz later wrote much, much more. Collecting folk tales for young people was a special interest.

More Books

Holland, Isabelle. *Dinah and the Green Fat Kingdom.* (HarperTrophy, 1978). A challenging book about a girl who invents a kingdom where fat people are the most beautiful.

Laurin, Anne. *Perfect Crane.* (Harper, 1981). A lonely Japanese magician creates a living crane out of paper and then must set it free.

Schwartz, Alvin. *Unriddling.* (HarperTrophy, 1983). Schwartz has collected riddles that will stimulate a reader's creativity.

LITERARY FOCUS

Figurative Language

Remind students that figurative language is the use of words beyond their usual or everyday meaning. For example, the author describes a night scene like this: ". . .when the moon is a giant orange in the sky. . . " The moon isn't really an orange, but the reader can picture what it looks like from the use of figurative language.

Activity: As students read, have them find an example of figurative language in the book, illustrate it, and share it with the class.

VOCABULARY STRATEGIES

Define the Critters

Kickle Snifters and Other Fearsome Critters describes some outlandish creatures. Students can select several creatures and write definitions for them. For example, a snawfus could be defined this way: a tree-top leaping white deer with flowered antlers. Its unusual call is "Halley-loo!"

A possible word list:
- glyptodont
- hoopajuba
- hugag
- wunk

Kickle Snifters

Literature Master 45
Use Prereading Strategies

Help students fill out the Reading Contract for *Kickle Snifters and Other Fearsome Critters*. Suggest students preview the table of contents and the illustrations. They should also read the Activity Card and select the activities for after reading. Students should feel free to amend their contracts as needed. *(preview; set purpose)*

Literature Master 46
Build Language and Concepts

Groups of students might discuss their favorite fanciful story creatures from childhood. Encourage students to bring the books to class if they still have them. **♦♦♦♦**
(activate prior knowledge)

Literature Master 47
Read Strategically

Kickle Snifters and Other Fearsome Critters introduces twenty-seven unusual creatures from American folklore. Literature Master 47 helps students classify the creatures. Accept their responses, encouraging them to support their ideas using examples from the book. ✎
(comprehension skill: classify)

Literature Master 48
Share and Discuss

Encourage open response after students have read the book. Literature Master 48, the Book Chat Guide, can be used by students to jot down their ideas about the creatures, their names, and who may or may not have seen them. Encourage students to discuss other creatures they may have heard or read about during their book chat. 💬 👤
(speaking and listening)

EEk2 Comprehension Strategies (Bi) Set an appropriate purpose for reading and/or listening
EEk1 Speaking (Bv) Share information

EEk2 Literary Appreciation (Div) Appreciate the use of sound devices and figurative language as they contribute to meaning
NAPT Reading Comprehension Interpret figurative language

Assess / Wrap up

■ CHECK ON THE READING ■

Conference with students after they finish reading *Kickle Snifters and Other Fearsome Critters*. Suggest that they review their critter classification chart. These questions might help you assess students' understanding of the book:

- What are the origins of all of these creatures? *(Do students realize that these imaginary creatures are from American folklore? that they were made up to entertain others?)*

- Which creature is your favorite? Why? *(Do students express their opinions and support them with facts?)*

- What might you find if you went in the woods near your house? *(Are students able to create a fearsome critter for their own area or match one from the book?)*

(See also Assessment Check in the BookFestival assessment component.)

Activity Card 12
Respond (Side 1)

Activity Card 12 provides a prompt for students' personal response to *Kickle Snifters*. Students choose their favorite critter and share it with the class. Remind students to keep the tone humorous.
(critical and creative thinking)

The Activity Card suggests these ideas:

1. **Write a Story** Students write a story about the discovery of their creature. ◄■■►
   (narrative writing)
2. **Interview a Creature** Pairs of students act out a talk show interview of the creature. **††**
   (dramatize)
3. **Launch a Campaign** Students make an endangered species poster for their creature.
   (persuasive writing)

Activity Card 12
Language Arts Connection (Side 2)

Students can work together to make a Kickle Snifter Zoo. Using their ideas, they can make models of the creatures and a catalog describing the care and feeding of each one.
(respond creatively)

The Activity Card suggests these ideas:

1. **Models** Using soft sculpture or some other medium, students make models of their creatures.
   (visualize)
2. **Illustrated Catalog** Students illustrate the critters, write instructions for their care and feeding, and compile the information into a book. **††††**
   (visualize, informative writing)
3. **Zoo Map** Students make a map of the Kickle Snifter Zoo.
   (use graphic sources)

EEk1 Speaking (Biii) Entertain others with stories, poems, and dramatic activities
EEk3 Writing (Draft) (Bv) Write in a variety of literary forms

EEk2 Literary Appreciation (Dv) Participate in cooperative learning and a variety of oral activities to elicit meaning from written text
EEk3 Writing (Draft) (Bii) Write narratives to tell stories and to inform in chronological order

ASSESS STUDENTS' ACTIVITIES

- **Respond:** Do students expand on the information in the book and bring these creatures to life?

- **Language Arts Connection:** Do students' zoos, catalogs, and maps reflect accurate descriptions of the creatures as well as creativity in rounding out these characters?

- **Connect Home and School:** Invite students to read their favorite chapters to their family. Then family members can invent and name household creatures that lurk in their house, for example, the one-sock gulper that raids the washing machine.

The Case of the Sabotaged School Play
by Marilyn Singer

• HIGHLIGHTS •

☑ average reading

Booktalk

This book will appeal to students who ...
- *like "who-done-its,"*
- *are ready for another Sam and Dave mystery.*

Resources

◆ Activity Card 13

✪ Literature Masters 49–52

✪ Writing Master 13

Themes

Core Theme:
Being a Close Observer

Related Themes:
Mysteries
Discoveries
Investigations

Content

Literary Focus:
Plot

Vocabulary Strategies:
Job-Related Words

Read Strategically:
Cause and Effect

Respond:
Be Part of the Mystery

Fine Arts Connection:
Be a Playwright

Choose As You Need

MEETING INDIVIDUAL NEEDS

Students who are at risk might work in a group and read the book aloud. ♦♦♦♦
Students with special needs might enjoy discussing the clues as they occur in the story. 💬 "🧍
Students who are achieving English proficiency might need background discussion on putting on a play. 💬 "🧍
Students who enjoy challenges might enjoy reading other mysteries by Marilyn Singer and comparing the plots.

Multicultural Connection

Intercultural Communication

Point out that the students in *The Case of the Sabotaged School Play* made fun of Mary Ellen Moseby because they didn't appreciate swashbuckling pirate stories. Ask students if they, too, are sometimes quick to judge a piece of music or a work of art or a type of literature because it is different from what is popular. Have students sample different types of music—gospel, salsa, reggae, classical, and so on—and talk about them in class. "🧍 💬

Summary

Someone wants to sabotage the school play The Merry Pirates. *The Bean brothers, Sam and Dave, piece the clues together, look for motives, and eventually solve the mystery.*

What Happens

Fake snake is planted in Donna's desk.
Scripts are torn up.
Chandelier falls.
Skunk smell is planted on stage.
Lights are fixed to black out.
Firecrackers go off on stage.

Suspects & Motives

Ginger would like to be in the play.
Joel hates the play; wants to do *Grease*.

Saboteur

Mary Ellen Moseby, the playwright, wants publicity for her play.

The Author

Until Marilyn Singer began to write mysteries, she would merely begin writing and see where the story led. When she began to write mysteries, she had to learn how to outline a good strong plot first, then write her story. She has written a series of Sam and Dave Bean mysteries. She has also written scripts for the "Electric Company" television series. However, more than anything else, Ms. Singer most enjoys writing poetry.

More Books

Cobb, Vicki. *How to Really Fool Yourself: Illusions for All Your Senses.* (Lippincott, 1981). Mirages and optical illusions mingle as dozens of stunts, sound effects, and mysteries are explained.

Fleischman, Paul. *Shadow Play.* (Harper, 1990). A puppet play of *Beauty and the Beast* is the background for this tale. Those who dare will open their eyes to giant shadows stalking the stage as they see how the verbal-visual pieces of this puzzle come together.

LITERARY FOCUS

Plot

Remind students that plot is the series of events that take place in a story. The plot in a mystery story is usually suspenseful, with each event building to the conclusion of the story when the mystery is solved.

Activity: Students can work in pairs to list the major events in *The Case of the Sabotaged School Play* and then rewrite them on a graphic organizer of their design to show the rising action in the story.

VOCABULARY STRATEGIES

Defining Job-Related Words

The Case of the Sabotaged School Play discusses many aspects of play production. Students can choose a theater job they might want and define the terms that they would need to know to do the job. The words *set*, *backdrop*, and *strobe* might be on the list for a stage crew member.

A possible word list for a stage crew:

- set
- backdrop
- strobe

Sabotaged School Play

Literature Master 49
Use Prereading Strategies

Help students fill out the Reading Contract for *The Case of the Sabotaged School Play*. Suggest students preview the illustrations and read the back cover of the book. They should also read the Activity Card to select activities for after reading. Students should feel free to amend their contracts as needed.

(preview; set purpose)

 ### Literature Master 50
Build Language and Concepts

Groups of students might use their mystery-solving charts to discuss real-life mysteries that they have solved. Encourage students to keep track of clues as they read *The Case of the Sabotaged School Play*. ♦♦♦♦

(activate prior knowledge)

 ### Literature Master 51
Read Strategically

The Case of the Sabotaged School Play is a mystery. Someone is pulling pranks that almost ruin the production of *The Merry Pirates*. Literature Master 51 helps readers keep track of the clues and the suspects as they try to solve the mystery along with Sam and Dave Bean.

(comprehension skill: cause and effect)

 ### Literature Master 52
Share and Discuss

Encourage open response after students have read groups of chapters or after they've completed the book. Students can use this page to jot down questions or comments as they try to solve the mystery. You might want to discuss basic elements of a mystery—clues, suspects, and motives—during the initial book chat.

(speaking and listening)

EEk2 Comprehension Strategies (Bi) Set an appropriate purpose for reading and/or listening
TAAS Reading Comprehension Analyze information in a variety of written texts in order to make inferences and generalizations (use graphic sources)

EEk2 Speaking (Bv) Share information
NAPT Reading Comprehension Understand cause and effect

Assess / Wrap Up

■ **CHECK ON THE READING** ■

Have conferences with students after they finish reading *The Case of the Sabotaged School Play*. They might refer to their clue sheets to remind them of events in the story. These questions might help you assess students' understanding of the story:

- What is the problem with Mary Ellen Moseby's plays? *(Do students realize that no one likes her plays and that no one goes to see them except parents of cast members?)*

- Who was your prime suspect in this case? Why? *(Do students understand the concept of "motive"?)*

- Were you surprised at the identity of the saboteur? Were you satisfied with the ending of this book? *(Can students express their opinions and support them with facts from the book?)*

(See also Assessment Check in the BookFestival assessment component.)

Activity Card 13
Respond (Side 1)

Activity Card 13 provides a prompt for students' personal response to *The Case of the Sabotaged School Play*. Students become part of the story by assuming the role of one of the characters. Remind students to speak and write from their character's point of view.
(critical and creative thinking)

The Activity Card suggests these ideas:
1. **Talk About You** Students prepare and give monologues as characters from the selection.
   (characterization)
2. **Picture It** Students draw scenes from the story that include favorite characters.
   (visualize)
3. **Keep a Casebook** Students become Sam or Dave and keep track of clues. ◀▬▬▣▷
   (informative writing)

Activity Card 13
Fine Arts Connection (Side 2)

After reading about play production, students can try writing, producing, and performing a play by themselves. Remind them to avoid Mary Ellen Moseby's mistake and choose a topic that will appeal to the audience!
(respond to literature in a variety of ways)

The Activity Card suggests these ideas:
1. **Write It Down** Students write a script for their play, including stage directions. ◀▬▬▣▷
   (literary writing)
2. **Get Set** Students plan the set for their play.
   (descriptive writing)
3. **Costume Design** Students sketch the costumes of major characters and include a written description of each character's costume. ◀▬▬▣▷
   (visualize)

EEk1 Speaking (Biii) Entertain others with stories, poems, and dramatic activities
EEk2 Comprehension Strategies (Biv) Develop inferential meaning by analyzing a variety of texts

EEk2 Literary Appreciation (Dv) Participate in cooperative learning and a variety of oral activities to elicit meaning from written text.
EEe3 Fine Arts (B) Dramatize literary selections using shadow play, pantomime, creative dialogue, improvisation, characterization, and puppetry

ASSESS STUDENTS' ACTIVITIES

- **Respond:** Do students show that they understand the motivations of the characters in the story?

- **Fine Arts Connection:** Do students demonstrate the creativity and organizational talents necessary to put on a play?

WRAP UP

- **Connect Home and School:** Invite family members to a production of an original play written, produced, and performed by the class.

Sabotaged School Play

From Anna

by Jean Little

☑ average reading

Booktalk

This book will appeal to students who ...
- *enjoy reading historical fiction,*
- *love stories about courageous people.*

Resources

- ◆ Activity Card 14
- ✪ Literature Masters 53–56
- ✪ Writing Master 14

Themes

Core Theme:
Standing Up for Your Beliefs

Related Themes:
Families
Immigrants
Overcoming Challenges

Content

Literary Focus:
Mood

Vocabulary Strategies:
What's the Mood?

Read Strategically:
Draw Conclusions

Respond:
Step into the Story

Science Connection:
Become an Expert

Choose As You Need

MEETING INDIVIDUAL NEEDS

Students who are at risk might enjoy discussing people they know who have shown courage. 💬
Students with special needs might benefit by making paper representations of story characters and dramatizing portions of the story. 💬 🎭
Students who are achieving English proficiency might discuss similarities between their own experiences and those of Anna when she had to speak a new language in a new country. 💬
Students who enjoy challenges might research and report on awards given for courageous acts.

Multicultural Connection

Community Culture

Students might enjoy finding out the ethnic make-up of their community or state. Where did the people originally come from? What unique traditions did they bring with them that have been passed down through generations? What community celebrations reflect ethnic backgrounds? Students may present their findings in a chart or web format. ✏️

Summary

Anna faces many challenges in her young life. In 1930s Germany, she has difficulty learning in school, and she's clumsy. When her family moves to Canada, an observant doctor and a caring teacher make a difference in her life. Her vision problems are treated and she becomes a more independent and respected person.

In Germany: There is general unrest as personal rights and freedoms are taken away. Anna is not treated well in school or at home, except by her father.

In Canada: Anna's visual problem is diagnosed. She starts wearing glasses and attends a school where she is finally accepted and feels successful.

Anna Solden

At home in Canada: Anna slowly comes out of her shell and becomes a stronger, more assertive, and more respected member of the Solden family.

The Author

Jean Little was born with only partial vision. Because of her sensitivity to physical challenges, she felt a need to write books for children that accurately depict challenged children. Her characters learn to deal with their limitations. They do not suddenly become cured. Many of Ms. Little's childhood experiences are reflected in *From Anna*.

More Books

Olson, Arielle North. *The Lighthouse Keeper's Daughter*. (Little, Brown, 1987). Miranda's family is new to the hard life at the island lighthouse. When Miranda's father is stranded away from the island, she shows extraordinary courage keeping the lighthouse lights burning to protect her family and sailors at sea.

Crofford, Emily. *A Matter of Pride*. (Carolrhoda, 1991). Meg makes fun of her mother's worries until she realizes that sometimes bravery means overcoming our greatest fears.

LITERARY FOCUS

Mood

Remind students that a story's mood is created by the words the author uses. These words help the reader visualize the scene, and they create emotions and feelings. A story's mood can be serene, scary, funny, sad, and so on.

Activity: As students read *From Anna* they will find that the mood changes throughout. Students can use note cards to jot down each chapter's mood and list some of the words or phrases that helped them decide what that mood was.

VOCABULARY STRATEGIES

What's the Mood?

When *From Anna* begins, there is a tense mood. Words and phrases such as *troubled days*, *frightened*, *angry*, and *sharp command* reflect this mood. Students can list different mood words and have a partner name the mood they describe.

A possible word list describing a tense mood:

- troubled days
- frightened
- angry
- sharp command

From Anna

Literature Master 53
Use Prereading Strategies

Help students fill out the Reading Contract for *From Anna*. Suggest that students preview the illustrations and chapter titles. They might also skim the Activity Card to preview possible activities to do after they complete reading the book. They should feel free to amend the contract as needed.
(preview; set purpose)

Literature Master 54
Build Language and Concepts

Partners can discuss the problems they might encounter if they were to move to a new country where a language unknown to them is spoken. Then they can complete the comparison chart.
(activate prior knowledge)

Literature Master 55
Read Strategically

Anna's life changes in many ways when she moves from Germany to America. Literature Master 55 helps readers keep track of story events at different times in Anna's life.
(comprehension skill: draw conclusions)

Literature Master 56
Share and Discuss

Encourage open response after students have read *From Anna*. Literature Master 56 provides starter questions for literature groups. Students can also use this page to jot down questions or comments they wish to discuss. You might use the questions during your own conference with students as well.
(speaking and listening)

EEk2 Comprehension Strategies (Bi) Set an appropriate purpose for reading and/or listening
TAAS Reading Comprehension Analyze information in a variety of written texts (Use graphic sources)

EEk1 Listening (Ai) Focus attention on and listen to both adult and peer speakers during large and small group interactions
NAPT Reading Comprehension Identify aspects of mood, tone, style, or structure in a passage

---

Assess / Wrap Up

■ CHECK ON THE READING ■

Conference with students after they finish reading *From Anna*. Suggest that they use Literature Masters 54–56 to assist them in their chat. These questions might help you assess students' understanding of the story:

- Anna's poor vision causes her problems both at school and at home. What events in the story describe these difficulties? *(Do students indicate story events that describe Anna's difficulties?)*

- How do Anna's teachers, friends, and family members treat her? *(Do students verbalize the negative treatment Anna receives from everybody but her father?)*

- Is Anna's life different from yours? Describe similarities and differences. *(Are students able to verbalize how historical periods affect the lives of individuals?)*

(See also *Assessment Check* in the *BookFestival* assessment component.)

Activity Card 14
Respond (Side 1)

Activity Card 14 prompts students' personal response to *From Anna*. Students become a member of Anna's family and step into a part of the story. They are to decide who they will be and what they will do and say.
(critical and creative thinking)

The Activity Card suggests these ideas:
1. **Write a Diary** Students write a diary entry describing their day with the Soldens. ✏️
   (descriptive writing)
2. **Talk About It** Students talk with friends about their day as a Solden family member. 👫💬
   (share information)
3. **Be a Poet** Students write a poem describing their feelings as a member of the Solden family.
   (expressive writing)

EEk1 Speaking (Bi) Use a variety of words to convey meaning
EEk3 Writing (Draft) (Bv) Write in a variety of literary forms

Activity Card 14
Science Connection (Side 2)

Students can become "experts" on how their sense of sight affects the way they perceive the world.
(use reference sources)

The Activity Card suggests these ideas:
1. **Draw a Diagram** Students diagram and label an eye and explain how it works.
   (organize information)
2. **Do Some Research** Students research and write a report on aides for visually challenged people. ✏️
   (informative writing)
3. **Find Optical Illusions** Students find and share optical illusions with a partner. 👫
   (use reference sources)

EEk2 Study Strategies (Ciii) Locate information using the dictionary, encyclopedia, and other library references
EEe4 Science (A) Obtain science information from varied resources

ASSESS STUDENTS' ACTIVITIES

- **Respond:** Do students show that they understand what it would have been like to be a member of the Solden family?

- **Science Connection:** Do students show an understanding of how the eye works and what helps people who have visual problems? Do they show an appreciation of how their eyes help them perceive the world?

WRAP UP

- **Connect Home and School:** Invite students to interview family members about people they know or have read about who have shown courage in dealing with life's challenges.

From Anna

The Adventures of Spider
retold by Joyce Cooper Arkhurst

• HIGHLIGHTS •

☑ average reading

Booktalk
This book will appeal to students who ...
- *enjoy reading folk tales,*
- *love Spider tales.*

Resources
◆ Activity Card 15
★ Literature Masters 57–60
★ Writing Master 15

Themes
Core Theme:
Courage in Folk Tales
Related Themes:
Animal Tales
Storytelling
Having Fun

Content
Literary Focus:
Folk Tales

Vocabulary Strategies:
Jungle Setting Words

Read Strategically:
Compare and Contrast

Respond:
Become Spider

Language Arts Connection:
Create a Story

Choose As You Need

MEETING INDIVIDUAL NEEDS

Students who are at risk might enjoy reading the stories with a partner. 👫
Students with special needs might make paper puppets of the story characters to use as they read or listen to the stories.
Students who are achieving English proficiency might benefit from more discussion about "How?" and "Why?" stories.
Students who enjoy challenges might want to make a classroom display of Spider stories or other folk tales.

Multicultural Connection

Cultural Perception
Students might enjoy finding a folk tale that is common to many different ethnic groups, such as Aesop tales or Cinderella stories. They might want to display these books for the class along with a chart that shows the similarities and differences between the tales.

Summary

In these six West African folk tales, mischievous Spider is sometimes greedy, lazy, and clever.

How Spider Got a Thin Waist
Spider ties two ropes around his waist. Following his orders, his sons pull the ropes, leaving Spider with a thin waist.

Why Spider Lives in Ceilings
Leopard plans to eat Spider. Clever Spider figures out the plan and hides on the ceiling.

How Spider Got a Bald Head
Greedy Spider hides boiling beans in his hat. His head burns, and he is forever bald.

How Spider Helped a Fisherman
Lazy Spider wants some of the fisherman's catch, but the fisherman tricks him into doing all the work.

Why Spiders Live in Dark Corners
Trickster Spider is caught again. Because of his shame, he hides in the dark corner.

How the World Got Wisdom
Spider keeps all wisdom in a clay pot. When his son has a good idea, Spider angrily shatters the pot and wisdom spreads all over the world.

The Author

Joyce Cooper Arkhurst is a librarian. As the wife of Ghana's former ambassador to the United Nations, she traveled to African nations where she collected many folk tales. Her first and second books, *The Adventures of Spider* and *More Adventures of Spider* retell some of these tales.

More Books

Lester, Julius. *How Many Spots Does a Leopard Have?* (Scholastic, 1989). This collection of African and Jewish folk tales includes tales of courageous and cunning acts by animals and people.

Anno, Mitsumasa. *Anno's Aesop.* (Orchard Books, 1987). When Freddy Fox finds a book of fables, his father reads it to him, but also makes up stories of his own. Both the classic versions of Aesop's fables and Mr. Fox's explanations of the same stories are included.

LITERARY FOCUS

Folk Tales
Remind students that folk tales originate with ordinary people and are passed down orally through generations. The characters are usually stereotypical: they have simple problems, and they express universal needs and wishes.

Activity: Students might enjoy making a classroom mural of their favorite folk tale characters. ♦♦♦♦

VOCABULARY STRATEGIES

Jungle Setting Words
The six stories in *The Adventures of Spider* take place in a jungle setting. Students can keep track of these related words and phrases and use them to create an illustration of the setting for one of the stories. The phrases *rainy season*, *tall grasses*, and *banana leaves* describe some of the jungle features.

A possible word list:
- rainy season
- tall grasses
- banana leaves

The Adventures of Spider

Literature Master 57
Use Prereading Strategies

Help students fill out the Reading Contract for *The Adventures of Spider*. Suggest students preview illustrations and story titles. They might also skim the Activity Card to preview activities for after reading. They should feel free to amend the contract as needed.
(preview; set purpose)

 Literature Master 58
Build Language and Concepts

Students answer letters to Spider from children. These letters ask Spider "How?" and "Why?" questions about his web, his thin waist, his eight legs, and walking up walls. Encourage students to write serious or silly answers to the questions. ◄▬▬►
(activate prior knowledge)

 Literature Master 59
Read Strategically

The Adventures of Spider contains six different stories about Spider. Literature Master 59 helps readers compare and contrast characters, settings, important events, and endings in three of the stories. Suggest that students might want to make another chart for the remaining three stories. ◄▬▬►
(comprehension: compare and contrast)

 Literature Master 60
Share and Discuss

Encourage open responses after students have read each tale or after they complete reading the book *The Adventures of Spider*. Literature Master 60 provides questions to help literature groups to start their book chats. ♀ ◝▪
(speaking and listening)

EEk2 Comprehension Strategies (Bi) Set an appropriate purpose for reading and/or listening
TAAS Reading Comprehension Identify supporting ideas in a variety of written texts (Describe character)

EEk2 Comprehension Strategies (Biii) Develop global meaning by analyzing a piece of text
NAPT Reading Comprehension Infer the traits, feelings, and motivations of characters

■ **CHECK ON THE READING** ■

Conference with children after they finish reading *The Adventures of Spider*. Suggest that they use their story maps or Book Chat Guide masters as aides. These questions might help you assess their understanding:

• Which "How?" or "Why?" story do you think is the most clever? Why? *(Do students indicate which story they feel is most clever? Do they give appropriate reasons for their choice?)*

• If you could be any character in one of the Spider stories, which one would you be? Why? *(Do students choose one character and tell why they made their choice?)*

• If you had to describe Spider to a friend, what would you say about him? *(Do students capture the lazy, mischievous, clever characterization of Spider?)*

(See also Assessment Check in the BookFestival assessment component.)

Activity Card 15
Respond (Side 1)

Activity Card 15 prompts students' personal response to *The Adventures of Spider*. Students become Spider. They are to choose the story with the most clever plan. As Spider, they can't understand why their plans usually fail.

(critical and creative thinking)

The Activity Card suggests these ideas:

1. **Write in a Diary** Students write a diary entry describing their plan and what they would try next time.
(descriptive writing)

2. **Draw a Cartoon** Students draw a cartoon story of the steps and results of their clever plan.
(visualize)

3. **Talk About a Plan** Students tell a friend their plan and find a way to make the plan more successful.

(share information)

EEk1 Speaking (Bv) Share information
EEk2 Literary Appreciation (Dv) Participate in cooperative learning and a variety of oral activities to elicit meaning from written text

 ## Activity Card 15
Language Arts Connection (Side 2)

Students brainstorm and write "How?" or "Why?" questions about their world, and then create a story using one of the topics. Students may work with a partner or small group.

(write in a variety of modes)

The Activity Card suggests these ideas:

1. **Write Your Story** Students write a story for the topic they choose.
(expressive writing)

2. **Plan a Puppet Show** Students plan a puppet show to tell their story.
(entertain)

3. **Share a Story** Students read or tell a "How?" or "Why?" story to a younger group of children. They may draw posters to accompany the story.
(consider purpose and audience)

EEk1 Speaking (Biii) Entertain others with stories, poems, and dramatic activities
EEk2 Study Strategies (Ci) Follow written directions

ASSESS STUDENTS' ACTIVITIES

- **Respond:** Do students show that they understand the clever plan in the story they choose?

- **Language Arts Connection:** Do students' stories demonstrate appropriate tellings of "How?" or "Why?" story formats?

 ### WRAP UP

- **Connect Home and School:** Invite students to share a folk tale with family members. What was their reaction? What folk tales do they remember and like?

Your Ideas

Reading Contract

I _____ agree to read *The Girl*
your name

Who Loved the Wind. I want to read this book because

_____

Write your own purpose for reading here.

_____

	Date you think you'll finish	**Date you did finish**
I plan to read *The Girl Who Loved the Wind* by:		
I would like to do Respond activity 1 2 3 (Circle your choice.)		
I would like to do Project Time activity 1 2 3 (Circle your choice.)		

Signed,

_____
signature and date

✏ **SOMETHING EXTRA**

Journal Idea While you read, jot down some words and phrases that describe what the wind is like. Tell how you feel about the wind as you read this story.

Name _____

Tell What Makes You Happy

Do you know what makes you happy? Write down some of the people, events, and things in your life that bring you happiness.

Things That Make Me Happy

Not everyone finds happiness the same way. Decide which of the choices below would be right for you and put a checkmark next to them. Then compare your ideas about happiness with those of your classmates.

Would you be happier . . .		
☐ if people you cared about always smiled and only told you good things?	**OR**	☐ if people you cared about told you how they really felt about things?
☐ if people gave you everything you wanted when you asked for it?	**OR**	☐ if you worked hard and earned the things you wanted?
☐ if your life followed the same peaceful routine day after day?	**OR**	☐ if every day brought a new and unexpected adventure?
☐ if you lived in a lovely palace but could never leave it?	**OR**	☐ if you traveled all over the world but never had any toys or books?

Think As You Read

Name _____

Create a Story Triangle

Follow the directions to complete your story triangle.
1. Name of the main character
2. Two words that describe the main character
3. Three words that describe the setting
4. Four words that tell what happens first
5. Five words that tell what happens next
6. Six words that tell what happens last

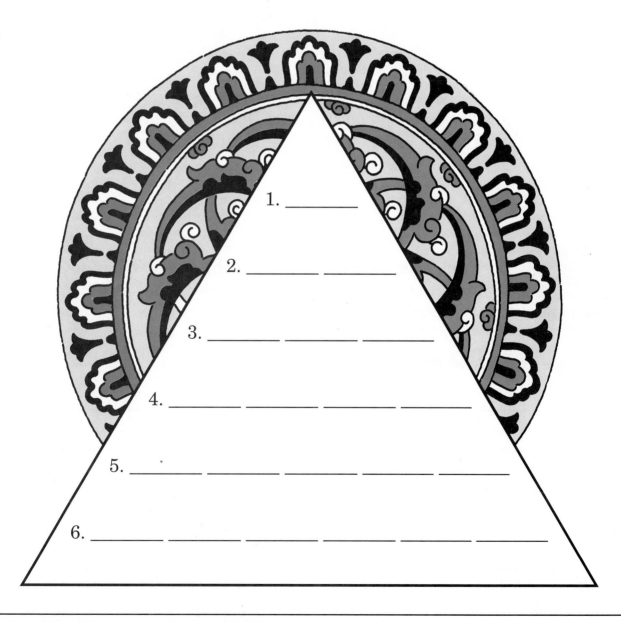

1. _____

2. _____ _____

3. _____ _____ _____

4. _____ _____ _____ _____

5. _____ _____ _____ _____ _____

6. _____ _____ _____ _____ _____ _____

Discuss What You've Read

Name _____

Book Chat Guide

After reading *The Girl Who Loved the Wind*, you may wish to discuss the story with others. Use the questions below and your own questions to begin a group discussion.

Chat About Plot

Why do you think Danina went with the wind? What could Danina's father have done differently in this story?

Chat About Character

How do you feel about the way Danina's father treated her? What would you do if you were treated as she was?

Chat About Art

Look back over the illustrations in this story. What do you think the artist was trying to show? What mood do the illustrations express?

Things You Want to Talk About

_____

_____

_____

_____

Reading Contract

I _____ agree to read *The*
your name

Mouse and the Motorcycle. My purpose in reading is

_____

Write your own purpose for reading here.

_____

I plan to read *The Mouse and the Motorcycle:*	Estimated completion date	Actual completion date
☐ straight through		
☐ in groups of chapters		
Chapters 1–4		
Chapters 5–7		
Chapters 8–10		
Chapters 11–13		
I plan to do these activities from the Activity Card:		
Respond, number _____		
Project Time, number _____		

_____   _____
     signature   *date*

 S O M E T H I N G   E X T R A

Journal Idea Imagine that you are the incredible
shrinking fourth grader! You are now the size of a
mouse. Write about the advantages and disadvantages
of being mouse-sized in a human-sized world.

Before You Read

Name _____

Write About Being Small

You are a tiny mouse in a house full of people! You must get everything you need from these people. You must keep yourself alive! How will you do it? Describe how you would solve the problems listed below.

You need a way to carry water to your nest.	You need something soft to sleep on.
The family cat sleeps next to the door of your nest.	You need food.

Mousetraps with great-tasting cheese are placed right outside your door.

Think As You Read

Name _____

Fill in a Time Line

Ralph the mouse only spends four days with Keith, but he manages to pack a lot into their time together! As you read the story, keep track of the action by filling in the time line below. Show the main events that happen each day and night of Keith's stay at the Mountain View Inn.

First Day (Friday)	Second Day (Saturday)	Third Day (Sunday)	Fourth Day (Monday)

First Night	Second Night	Third Night

Name _____

Book Chat Guide

You may want to share your reactions to *The Mouse and the Motorcycle* with others after you read each group of chapters, and again after you finish the book. The questions in the boxes will help get your group talking. Write your own questions for discussion as you read.

Chapters 1–4

Chat About Genre

After reading Chapter 1, you might think that this book is realistic fiction. When do you know it is not? How do you know?

Your Own Questions

_____

_____

Chapters 5–7

Chat About Plot

Ralph breaks his promise to Keith when he rides the motorcycle during the day. What would you have done if you were Ralph?

Your Own Questions

_____

_____

Chapters 8–10

Chat About Character

Compare Ralph and Keith. How are they alike? How are they different?

Your Own Questions

_____

_____

_____

Chapters 11–13

Chat About Conflict

What dangers does Ralph face as he tries to help Keith?

Your Own Questions

_____

_____

_____

Reading Contract

I _____ agree to read *There's a*

your name

Boy in the Girls' Bathroom. My purpose for reading is

_____

Write your own purpose for reading here.

_____

I plan to *(Check one.)*

☐ read the book in one sitting.

☐ read the book in groups of chapters.

Chapters 1–11

Chapters 12–23

Chapters 24–35

Chapters 36–47

I will finish reading the book by *(Fill in the date.)*

I also agree to complete these activities from Activity Card 3. *(Circle one from each category.)*

Respond 1 2 3

Project Time 1 2 3

Signed,

_____

signature and date

✎ S O M E T H I N G   E X T R A

Journal Idea How embarrassing it would be to walk into the wrong bathroom! What's your most embarrassing moment? Write about it. How did you feel about it then? How do you feel about it now?

Before You Read

Name _____

Write Solutions to School Problems

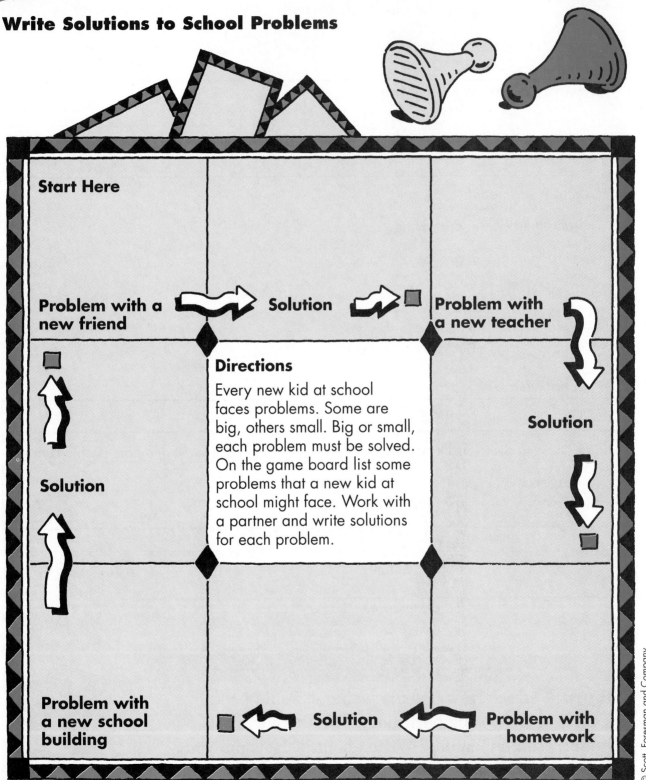

Start Here

Problem with a new friend → **Solution** → **Problem with a new teacher**

Solution

Directions

Every new kid at school faces problems. Some are big, others small. Big or small, each problem must be solved. On the game board list some problems that a new kid at school might face. Work with a partner and write solutions for each problem.

Solution

Problem with a new school building

Solution

Problem with homework

Name _____

Show How Characters Feel About Each Other

Bradley changes from unlikeable to almost likeable in *There's a Boy in the Girls' Bathroom*. On the diagram below, draw lines to connect characters from the story. On the lines, write how these characters feel about each other.

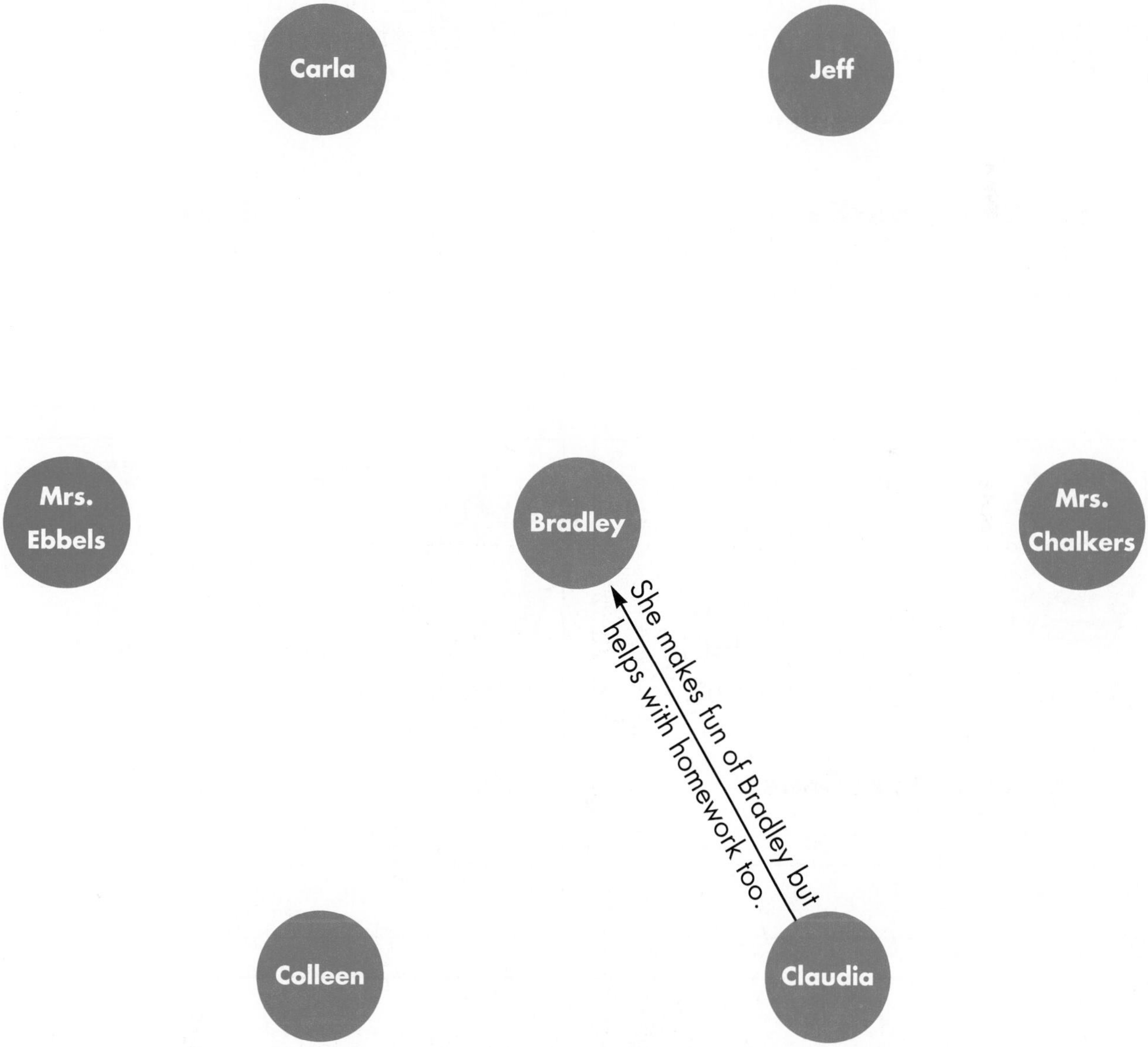

Carla

Jeff

Mrs. Ebbels

Bradley

Mrs. Chalkers

She makes fun of Bradley but helps with homework too.

Colleen

Claudia

Discuss What You've Read

Name _____

Book Chat Guide

You may want to use the questions below for discussion after reading each group of chapters or after finishing the book.

Chat About Conflict

Chapters 1–11

The students at Red Hill School really need Carla Davis, the counselor. What are some of the problems they are experiencing?

Your Own Questions

_____

_____

Chat About Character

Chapters 12–23

Imagine you are Jeff. How would you describe Bradley to your parents?

Your Own Questions

_____

_____

Chat About Plot

Chapters 24–35

What are the major events in these chapters? What is the turning point in the novel? Why do you think so?

Your Own Questions

_____

_____

Chat About Endings

Chapters 36–47

Recall the problems different characters had. How are they resolved? Did you predict that the book would end this way?

Your Own Questions

_____

_____

Reading Contract

I _____ agree to read
your name

Night Markets. I plan to read *Night Markets* because

_____

Write your own purpose for reading here.

_____

I would like to read the book in the following way:	Date you think you'll finish	Date you did finish
☐ straight through		
☐ in groups of pages		
pages 7–33		
pages 34–51		
pages 53–73		
pages 74–91		
☐ I plan to do Respond activity 1 2 3 (Circle your choice.)		
☐ I plan to do Project Time activity 1 2 3 (Circle your choice.)		

Signed,

_____
signature and date

✎ **S O M E T H I N G   E X T R A**

Journal Idea Think about your favorite foods and how they travel from farm or lake or ocean to your table. Draw some diagrams to help you show your ideas.

Name _____

Diagram How Food Moves from Farm to Table

A bowl of wheat flakes and milk start out as grains of wheat from a farm and milk from a cow. What happens to the wheat and milk between the farm and your table? Draw a diagram to show your ideas.

Think As You Read

Name _____

Figure Out the Main Idea

What is *Night Markets* all about? As you read, jot down details you learn about what goes on at a big city market at night. (Make as many boxes as you need.) Then summarize the details in a sentence or two that tells the main idea of *Night Markets*. You can refer to your chart during your book chat if you wish.

Detail

Fruit and vegetables come by truck, plane, and ship.

Main Idea of *Night Markets*:

Discuss What You've Read

Name _____

Book Chat Guide

You may want to discuss *Night Markets* after you have read it. Here are some questions to get your discussion group started. You can write your own questions on the lines for the group to talk about.

Chat About the Book

Talk about what goes on in the markets.

• Did you read about a food or product you use? Where does it come from?

• Were you surprised that meat and fish are trimmed and cut up at the market? What else surprised you?

• Why do you think flowers and plants are sorted in a market along with meat and vegetables? Why does this make sense?

Your Own Questions or Things to Talk About

_____

_____

_____

Reading Contract

I _____ plan to read *Sidewalk*
your name

Story because I would like to find out

_____

Write your own purpose for reading here.

_____

_____

Fill in the rest of the contract telling your plan for reading *Sidewalk Story*.

How You'll Read These Pages	Date You Think You'll Finish	Date You Did Finish
☐ straight through		
☐ in groups of pages		
pages 7–31		
pages 32–49		
pages 50–72		
I plan to do Respond activity 1 2 3 (Circle your choice.)		
I plan to do Project Time activity 1 2 3 (Circle your choice.)		

Signed,

_____
your name

✎ **S O M E T H I N G E X T R A**

Journal Idea As you read, write down your feelings about what happens to the two girls in the story, Lilly Etta and Tanya. What would you have done in their place?

Name _____

Write About Helping a Friend

In *Sidewalk Story* one friend tries to help another through some difficult times. Think about a time when you helped a friend or a family member in some way. Fill in the details on the friendship circle below.

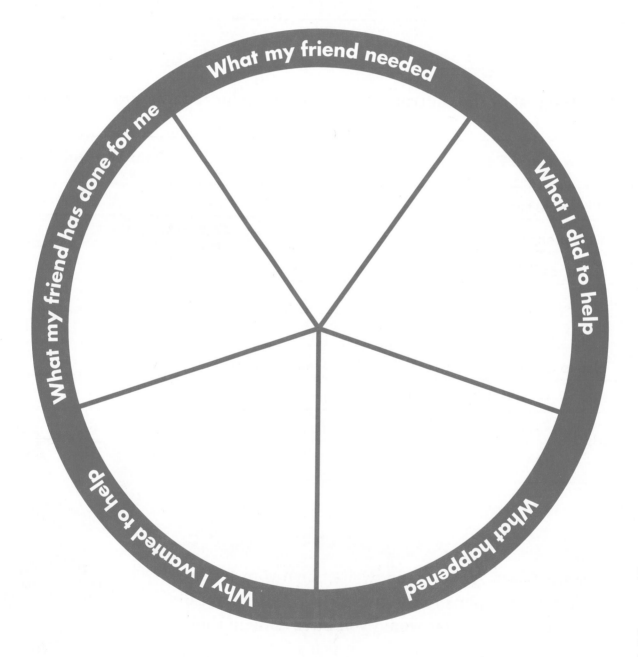

What my friend needed

What my friend has done for me

What I did to help

Why I wanted to help

What happened

Name _____

Make a Story Graph

Lilly Etta will do anything to help her friend Tanya. As you read this
story, think about which parts of it you find the most exciting. On the
story graph below, list important events from the story. Above each event,
mark a dot on the graph to show how exciting you thought the event was.
Then connect all the marked dots with a line. You may enjoy comparing
your story graph with a friend's.

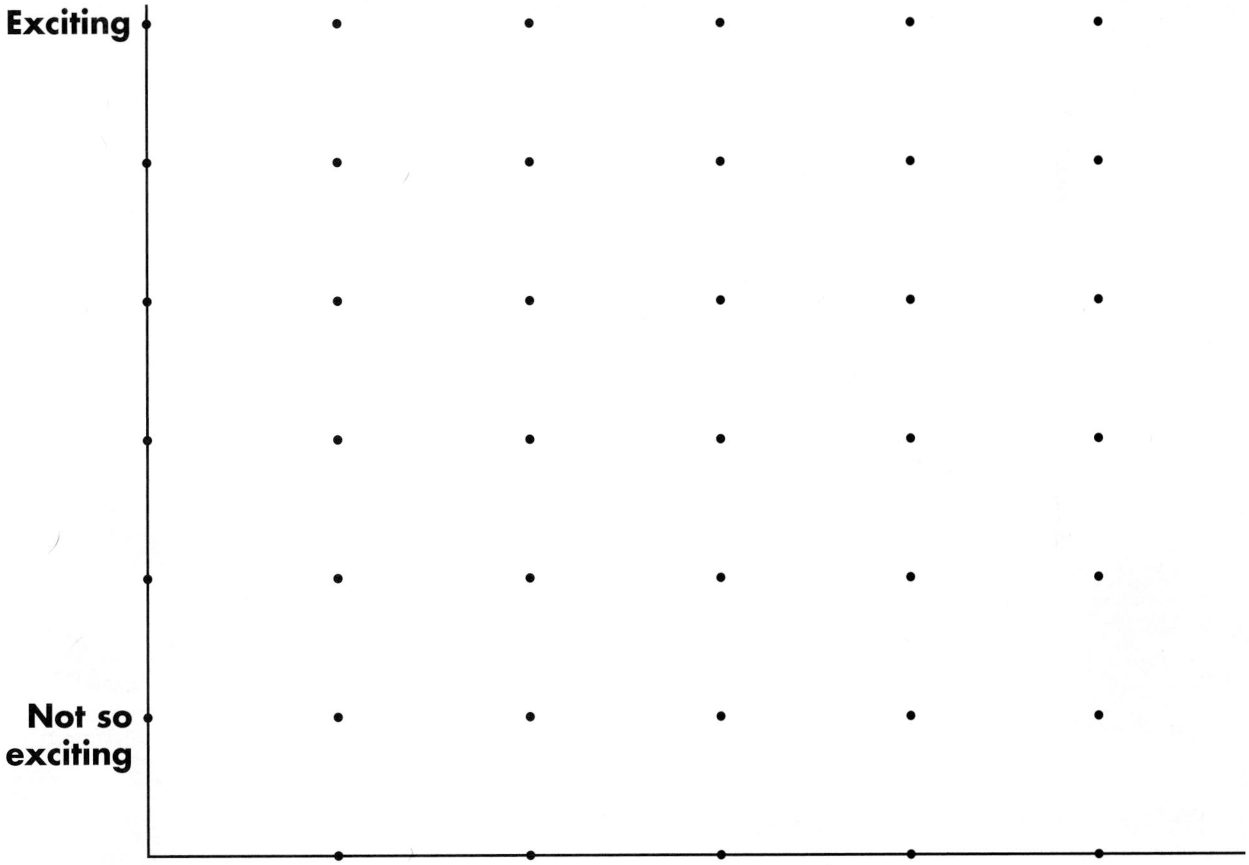

Exciting

**Not so
exciting**

**Main
Events**

Lilly Etta sees _____ _____ _____ _____

that Tanya is _____ _____ _____ _____

being evicted. _____ _____ _____ _____

_____ _____ _____ _____

Discuss What You've Read

Name _____

Book Chat Guide

You might want to talk about *Sidewalk Story* after you have read it. Here are some questions to get your discussion group started. You can write your own questions for the group to talk about on the lines.

Chat About Character

Talk about the girls in the story, Lilly Etta and Tanya. What gives you the idea they are close friends? What other characters do you remember? Why?

Things You Want to Talk About

_____

_____

_____

Chat About Theme

Does this story have a message for you? What do you think the author was trying to tell people by writing this story?

Things You Want to Talk About

_____

_____

_____

Reading Contract

I _____ agree to read *Tales of a*

your name

Fourth Grade Nothing. My purpose in reading is

_____

Write your own purpose for reading here.

I plan to (Check one.)
☐   read the book in one sitting
☐   read the book in groups of chapters:
Chapters 1–3
Chapters 4–5
Chapters 6–7
Chapters 8–10
I will finish reading the book by _____(Fill in the date.)

I also agree to complete these activities on Activity Card 6:
 (Circle one from each category.)
      Respond   1   2   3
      Project Time   1   2   3

_____   _____

signature   *date*

✎ S O M E T H I N G   E X T R A

Journal Idea Sometimes sisters or brothers can be a real nuisance! As you read about what Fudge does to his brother Peter, write down anything that reminds you of something that has happened to you.

Before You Read

Name _____

Write a Funny Story

Younger brothers and sisters can be fun, but they can also bring trouble!
Write a story about a time when you or someone you know had to deal
with a problem caused by a little brother or sister. You may want to share
your story with some of your classmates.

Think As You Read

Name _____

Fill Out a Cause-Effect Frame

Choose five episodes you like in *Tales of a Fourth Grade Nothing*. (An episode is a little story or event.) Fill out a cause-effect frame for each episode you choose. Share the episodes with someone else who has read this book. Which episodes did you both choose?

When Fudge Does This (Cause)	This Happens (Effect)

© Scott, Foresman and Company

Discuss What You've Read

Name _____

Book Chat Guide

You may want to talk about *Tales of a Fourth Grade Nothing* with others after you read each group of chapters, and again after you finish the book. You can use the questions in the boxes to help begin your discussion. Jot down your own questions as you read.

Chat About Setting

Chapters 1–3
Where does Peter Hatcher live? Can you describe his home? How does it compare to yours?

Your Own Questions

_____

_____

Chat About Character

Chapters 4–5
How would you describe Farley Drexel Hatcher? his brother? his mother?

Your Own Questions

_____

_____

Chat About Point of View

Chapters 6–7
Who narrates this book? Why do you suppose Judy Blume chose this narrator?

Your Own Questions

_____

_____

Chat About Character

Chapters 8–10
Living with Fudge isn't easy. What does Peter learn about himself and about his parents?

Your Own Questions

_____

_____

Reading Contract

I _____ do agree to read *Staying*
your name

Nine by Pam Conrad to find out _____

_____

Write your own purpose for reading here.

_____

My reading plan is to:	Date you think you'll finish	Date you did finish
☐ read the book straight through		
☐ read the book in groups of chapters		
Chapters 1–2		
Chapters 3–4		
Chapters 5–6		
☐ I also plan to do Respond activity 1 2 3 (Circle your choice.)		
☐ I plan to do Project Time activity 1 2 3 (Circle your choice.)		

Signed,

_____
signature and date

✏ S O M E T H I N G   E X T R A

Journal Idea Before reading, recall your favorite
birthday. Write about how you, your family, or your
friends celebrated that birthday. What made it special?
Brighten up your journal entry with an illustration!

© Scott, Foresman and Company

Name _____

Think About Your Age

Do you like the age you are right now? Is there another age you would rather be? On the chart below, fill in how old you are. Then list the things you do and don't like about being that age.

What I like about being	**What I don't like about being**
_____ *(Write your age here.)*	_____ *(Write your age here.)*

© Scott, Foresman and Company

Name _____

Make a Story Graph

What parts of this story do you think are the most exciting? On the story graph below, list the important events from the story. Above each event, mark a dot on the graph to show how exciting you thought the event was. Then connect all the marked dots with a line. What does your graph tell you about the story?

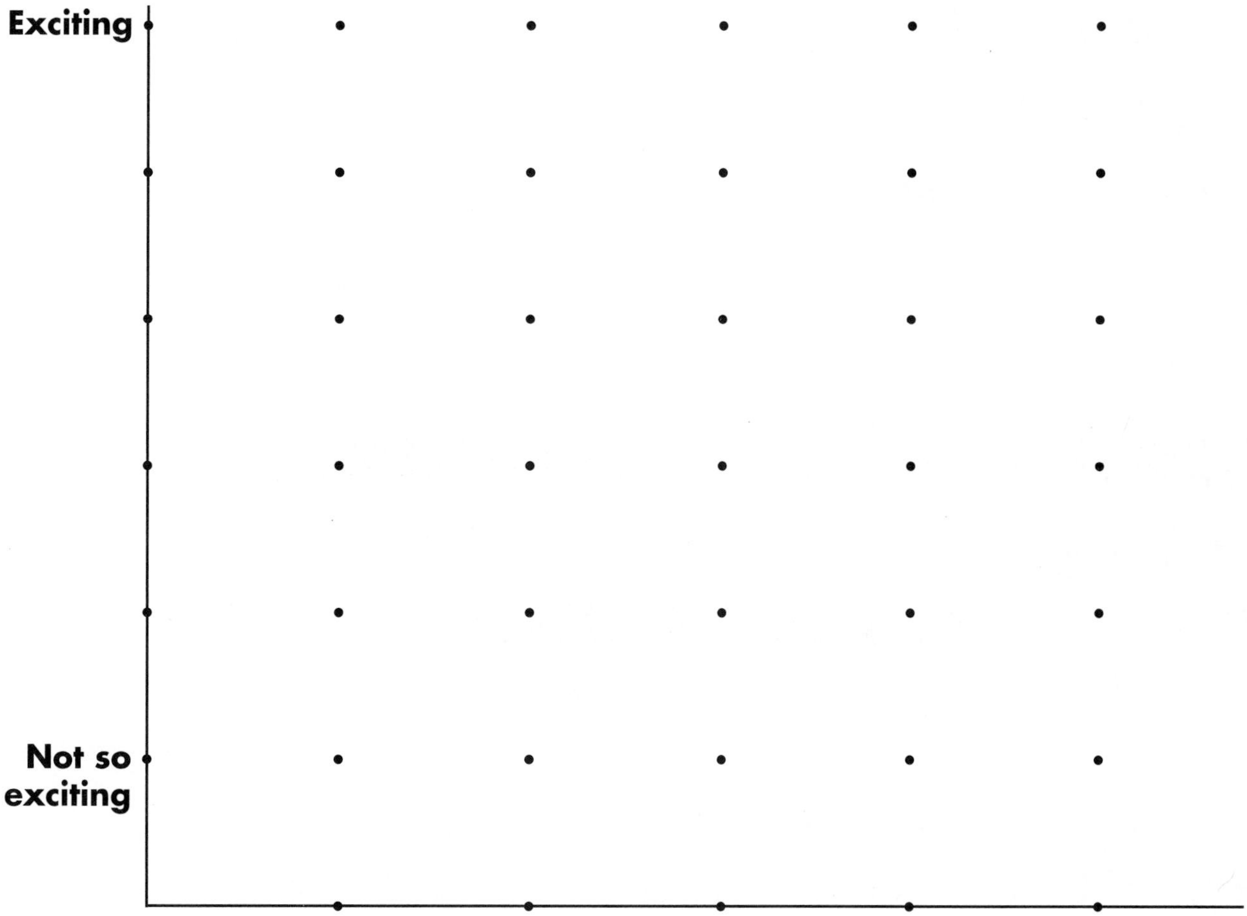

Exciting

Not so exciting

Main Events   Heather says _____ _____ _____ _____

she doesn't _____ _____ _____ _____

want a party. _____ _____ _____ _____

Name _____

Book Chat Guide

You may want to discuss *Staying Nine* after you read each group of pages or after you finish the book. Use the questions below and your own questions to get your group talking.

Chapters 1–2

What is Heather's big problem? How does it affect her behavior? How does her family react to her problem? What do you think about it?

Things You Want to Talk About

_____

Chapters 3–4

If "actions speak louder than words," what are Heather's actions saying?

Things You Want to Talk About

_____

Chapters 5–6

How do the other characters help Heather? What does Heather learn about herself on her tenth birthday?

Things You Want to Talk About

_____

Reading Contract

I _____ agree to read *Willie*
your name

Mays: Young Superstar. My purpose in reading is

_____

Write your own purpose here.

_____

I plan to read *Willie Mays: Young Superstar*
☐   straight through
☐   in groups of pages
pages 6–23
pages 24–48
I hope to finish by (give date) _____
I did finish by (give date) _____
I plan to do these activities on the Activity Card:
Respond activity number _____
Project Time activity number _____

Signed,

_____
signature and date

✎ S O M E T H I N G   E X T R A

Journal Idea Willie Mays has always been admired
for his high principles as well as his baseball-playing
abilities. As you read, make notes about the experiences
Willie Mays had that helped make him a good person
and a great baseball player.

Before You Read

Name _____

Find Out About Baseball

Batter up! There are nine playing positions on an official baseball team. Do you know what they are? If not, find someone who knows baseball well to help you. Write the name of each position on the line next to where it belongs on diagram. Don't forget the batter! Then use the diagram to show how the game is played.

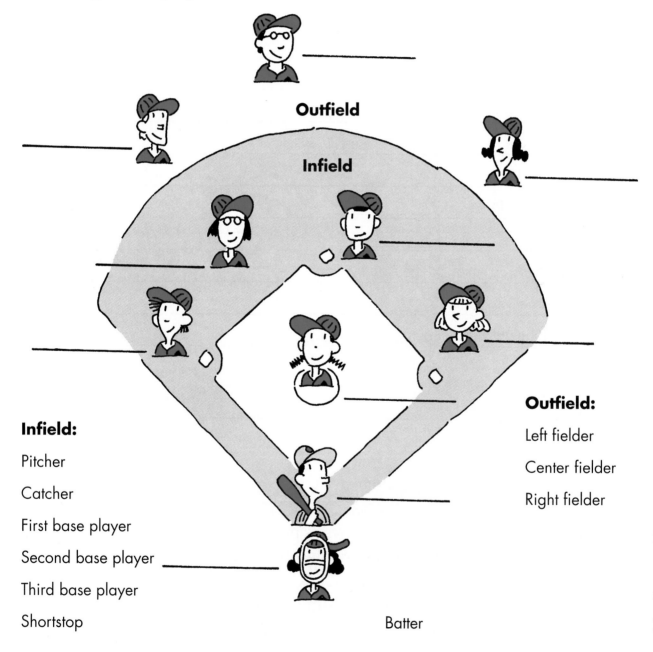

Infield:

Pitcher

Catcher

First base player

Second base player

Third base player

Shortstop

Outfield:

Left fielder

Center fielder

Right fielder

Batter

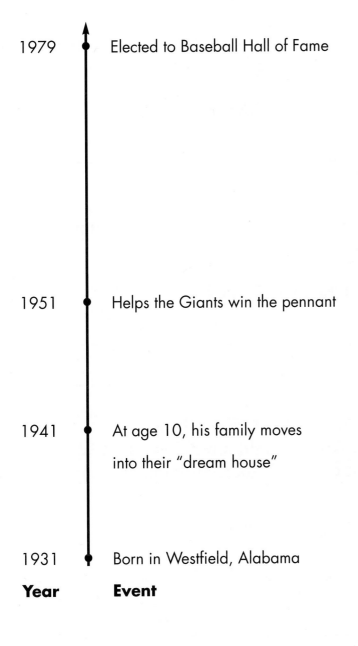

Think As You Read

Name _____

Make a Time Line

Willie Mays was only six months old when he first played with a ball. Add to the time line below to help you keep track of the events that influenced Willie Mays's life and his baseball career.

1979 ● Elected to Baseball Hall of Fame

1951 ● Helps the Giants win the pennant

1941 ● At age 10, his family moves

into their "dream house"

1931 ● Born in Westfield, Alabama

Year   **Event**

© Scott, Foresman and Company

Discuss What You've Read

Name _____

Book Chat Guide

You may want to discuss *Willie Mays: Young Superstar* with others after you have finished the book. You can use the questions below to get your group talking. As you read, add your own questions or topics for discussion.

Chat About Character

What was Willie Mays's father like? What do you think Willie learned from his father?

Things You Want to Talk About

_____

Chat About Family

How did Willie's family help him? Was Willie's family like any family that you know?

Things You Want to Talk About

_____

_____

Chat About Events

The book says Willie and his father never talked about the moment when Willie caught a ball his father would have missed. What do you think that moment meant to each of them?

Things You Want to Talk About

_____

_____

Reading Contract

I _____ agree to read *Esio Trot*.
your name

My purpose for reading is _____

Write your own purpose for reading here.

_____

_____

Fill in the rest of the contract telling how you will read the book, when you will finish reading it and what activities you will do.

I plan to read *Esio Trot*	Date I think I'll finish	Date I did finish
☐ straight through		
☐ in three parts		
pages 4–25		
pages 26–42		
pages 43–62		
☐ I would like to do Respond activity 1 2 3 (Circle your choice.)		
☐ I would like to do Project Time activity 1 2 3 (Circle your choice.)		

_____   _____
signature   *date*

✎ S O M E T H I N G   E X T R A

Journal Idea While you read, can you figure out what Mr. Hoppy's plan is? Write about what his plan might be and whether or not you think it will work.

Before You Read

Name _____

Tell How to Make a Friend

In *Esio Trot*, Mr. Hoppy wants to be friends with Mrs. Silver, but she doesn't even know he's alive. Have you ever met someone and wished that he or she could be your good friend? How could you convince that person that you would be a good friend to have? Think of the steps you would take to make a new friend. Write your plan of action in the boxes below.

How to Make a Friend

First, I would _____
_____
_____
_____

Next, I would _____
_____
_____
_____

Then, I would _____
_____
_____
_____

Name _____

Show How a Character Solves a Problem

Mr. Hoppy has a problem. Can he solve it? In the first turtle below, write down what Mr. Hoppy's problem is. In the second turtle, tell what he does to solve his problem. In the third turtle, tell what happens in the end. Does Mr. Hoppy solve his problem?

The Problem

The Action

The Result

Discuss What You've Read

Name _____

Book Chat Guide

You may want to discuss *Esio Trot* after you have read each group of pages and again after you have finished the book. You can use these questions to get your group talking. Write your own questions for discussion as you read.

Pages 4–25

Chat About Predicting

Mr. Hoppy seems to have a strange plan for making Alfie bigger. Do you think he's telling the truth? What do you think is really going to happen?

Your Own Questions

_____

_____

_____

Pages 26–42

Chat About Character

What have you learned about Mr. Hoppy? How would you describe him to someone who hasn't read the story?

Your Own Questions

_____

_____

_____

Pages 43–63

Chat About Plot

"All's well that ends well." What do you think of Mr. Hoppy's plan now? Did anything in this story surprise you? Explain.

Your Own Questions

_____

_____

_____

Reading Contract

I _____ do agree to read *Sarah,*
your name

Plain and Tall. My purpose for reading is

_____

Write your own purpose for reading here.

_____

I plan to read *Sarah, Plain and Tall*	Date I think I'll finish	Date I did finish
☐ straight through		
☐ in groups of chapters		
Chapters 1–3		
Chapters 4–9		
Activities I plan to do:		
☐ Activity Card: Respond activity 1 2 3 (Circle your choice.)		
☐ Activity Card: Project Time activity 1 2 3 (Circle your choice.)		

Signed,

_____
signature and date

✏ SOMETHING EXTRA

Journal Idea As you read, you might want to jot down notes about words that describe the prairie setting of the story. Also jot down what your feelings about the prairie are as you read the story.

Name _____

Create an Ad for Your Town

In the book you are about to read, *Sarah, Plain and Tall*, Sarah Wheaton reads an ad in her local newspaper that convinces her to move to a new town. What is wonderful and inviting about your town? Create an ad that would encourage someone to move to your town. In your ad, tell why a person coming to your town for the first time will be pleased and excited about living there. You might mention the weather, what your town looks like, or how people work and have fun.

aily News ★★★★

Move to Our Town

d
was
et
e will
on
ns.

n
ter
he
of
ch

the
has

Business News
Smith Manufacturing has given

Weather
Showers likely

Think As You Read

Name _____

Make a Comparison Chart

Will Sarah stay on the prairie? Or will she go back to Maine? As you read *Sarah, Plain and Tall* fill in each side of the chart. When you finish reading the story, compare Sarah's decision with what you might have done.

Reasons to Stay	Reasons to Go

© Scott, Foresman and Company

Discuss What You've Read

Name ____________________

Book Chat Guide

You may want to use the questions below for discussion after reading Chapters 1–3 and again after finishing the book.

Chat About Reasons

Chapters 1-3

Jacob, Anna, and Caleb each have unique reasons for wanting Sarah to come from Maine. What are their reasons? What do they worry about? What do you think Sarah worries about?

Your Own Questions

____

Chat About Events

Chapters 4-9

Throughout the story, there are clues that make you wonder whether or not Sarah will stay with the Wittings. What are these clues? Your Comparison Chart may be helpful.

Your Own Questions

____

Chat About Character

Jacob says that "Sarah is Sarah." How would you describe Sarah to a person who has not read the story?

Your Own Questions

____

Reading Contract

I _____ agree to read *Grandma*
your name

Moses: Painter of Rural America. My purpose for reading is

_____

Write your own purpose for reading here.

Fill in the rest of the contract telling how you will read the book, when you will finish reading it and what activities you will do.

I plan to read *Grandma Moses*	Date I think I'll finish	Date I did finish
☐ straight through		
☐ in groups of chapters		
Chapters 1–2		
Chapters 3–4		
Chapters 5–7		
I plan to do these activities from the Activity Card: Respond, number _____ Project Time, number _____		

_____   _____
signature   date

✎ SOMETHING EXTRA

Journal Idea For Grandma Moses, life in the country meant she never ran out of beautiful scenes to paint. As you read, keep a list of images described in the book that you would like to paint if you were Grandma Moses.

Name _____

Write About Artists and Their Work

What do you know about artists and how they work? Fill in the picture frames below with your ideas. Compare your ideas with those of your classmates. After you read *Grandma Moses*, you may discover more facts that you will want to add on this page.

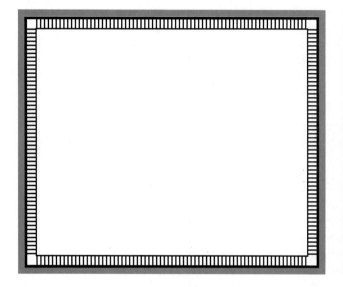

What do artists create?

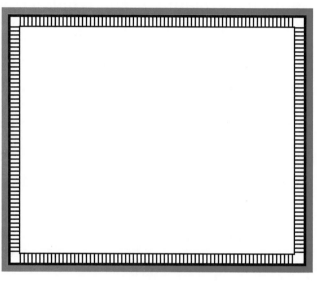

What materials do artists use?

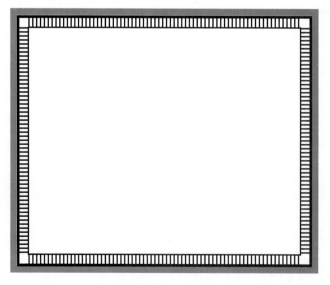

How do people become artists?

Name _____

Create a Details Web

A details web is a great way to keep track of facts and details when you read. Use the web below to write down details about the life and paintings of Grandma Moses. Use your web in your discussions of Grandma Moses.

The Life and
Paintings of
Grandma Moses

Name _____

Book Chat Guide

You may want to discuss *Grandma Moses* with others after you read each group of chapters, and again after you finish the book. You can use the questions below to get your group talking. Write your own questions or topics for discussion as you read.

Chapters 1–2

When Grandma Moses was a child, no one knew she would become a famous artist. Discuss whether or not Anna Mary showed her potential to be an artist when she was a little girl.

Chapters 3–4

What events influenced Grandma Moses to start painting? What could be some reasons why she didn't begin to paint regularly until she was seventy years old?

Chapters 5–7

When Grandma Moses became famous, how did her life change? What did she like and dislike about becoming well-known?

Things You Want to Talk About

_____

_____

_____

_____

Reading Contract

I _____ agree to read *Kickle*
your name

Snifters and Other Fearsome Critters. By reading, I hope
I find out

☐ who or what a Sickle Knitter is (I mean a Kickle Snifter) and

☐ _____

Write your own purpose for reading here.

Fill in the rest of the contract telling your plan for reading about Krickle
Sifters. (I mean Kickle Snifters!)

Reading These Pages	Date you think you'll finish	Date you did finish
Pages 8–19		
Pages 20–49		
Pages 50–61		
I would like to do Respond activity 1 2 3 (Circle your choice.)		
I would like to do Project Time activity 1 2 3 (Circle your choice.)		

Signed,

_____

signature and date

Is there really such a thing as a Krockle Sotter?

✎ **S O M E T H I N G   E X T R A**

Jokes As you read, write some jokes or riddles for your
friends about these fearsome critters. Can you top this?
Knock, Knock. Who's there? Wunk. Wunk who?
Wunk who come and play with me?

Before You Read

Name _____

Remember a childhood story about a horrible heffalump?* Maybe you still long for another book about a wild thing. Think back about your favorite story creatures (real or fanciful; nice or nasty). Draw one below and describe it. Share your creature with your classmates.

My Favorite Story Creature

_____

_____

_____

*Piglet battled a heffalump in *Winnie the Pooh*.

Name _____

Classify Fearsome Critters
Classify the fearsome critters you read about in *Kickle Snifters and Other Fearsome Critters*.

Fearsome Critters

Most Likely to Wake the Baby

Useful on a Camping Trip

You'd Like to Meet

You'd Run Away from Fast

Most Likely to Cheer You If You Feel Sad

© Scott, Foresman and Company

Name _____

Book Chat Guide

You might want to talk about *Kickle Snifters* after you have read it. Here are some questions to get your discussion group started. On the lines below, you can write your own questions for the group.

Chat About Funny Names

Talk about the names of the creatures. How do you think these creatures got their names? Which do you think are the silliest?

Things You Want to Talk About

_____

_____

_____

Chat About the Creatures

On the first page of *Kickle Snifters* we learn that "cowboys, woodsmen, hunters, and other people see these creatures again and again. Or say they do." When do you think these creatures might be seen? Have you ever heard of someone who has seen a "fearsome critter"?

Things You Want to Talk About

_____

_____

_____

Reading Contract

I _____ agree to read *The Case*
your name

of the Sabotaged School Play. My purpose for reading is

_____

Write your own purpose for reading here.

I plan to read *The Case of the Sabotaged School Play:*	Date you think you'll finish	Date you did finish
☐ straight through		
☐ in groups of chapters		
Chapters 1–4		
Chapters 5–8		
Chapters 9–12		
Chapters 13–16		
I plan to do these activities from the Activity Card:		
Respond, number ___		
Project Time, number ___		

Signed,

_____
signature and date

✏ S O M E T H I N G E X T R A

Journal Idea Jargon is a specialized vocabulary. As
you read, jot down words that are part of an actor's
jargon and words that are part of a detective's jargon.
Define them in your own words.

Before You Read

Name _____

Write About a Mystery You Have Solved

"Who ate the last piece of pizza?" "Why is my homework missing?" Real-life mysteries are all around us. You have probably solved many mysteries yourself, like where you left your lunch bag, or why your T-shirt turned blue when you washed it. Think of a mystery you have solved. Tell what the mystery was, what clues you found, and what the solution of your mystery was.

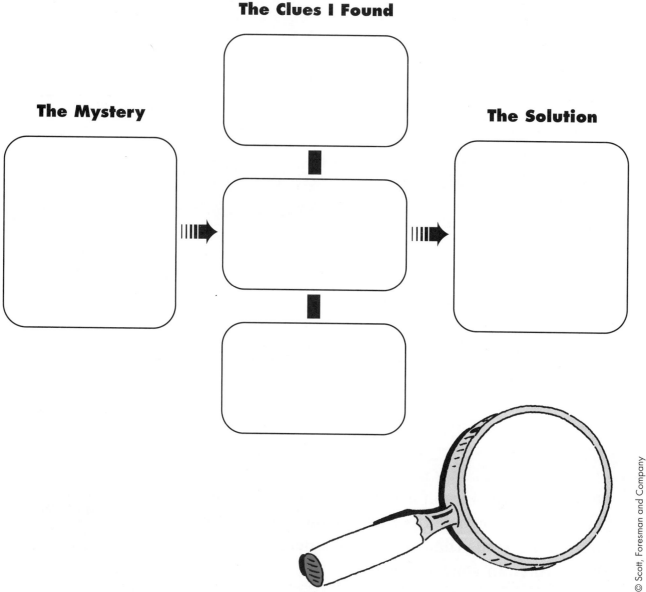

The Clues I Found

The Mystery

The Solution

Think As You Read

Name _____

Fill in Clues to a Mystery

Detectives Sam and Dave Bean are hot on the trail of the person who wants to ruin the school play. As you read, write down the names of the suspects you have and the clues that make you suspect them. Can you solve the mystery before Sam and Dave do?

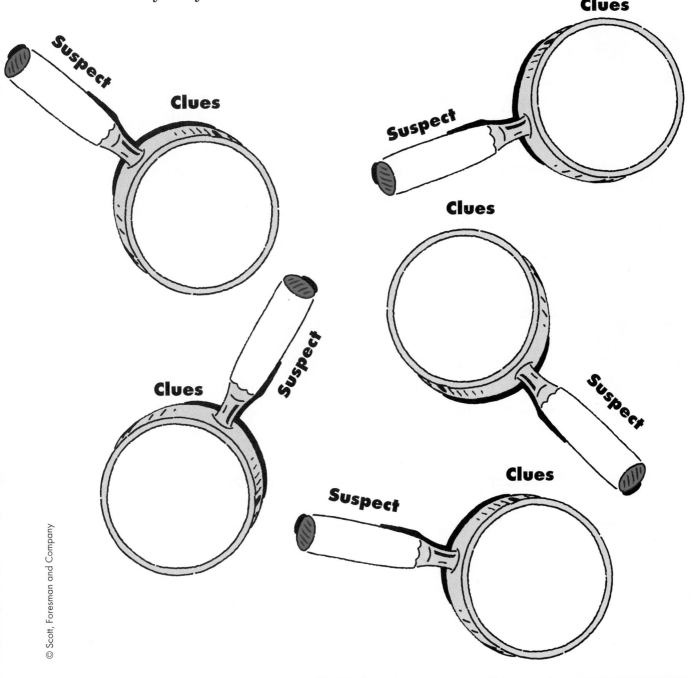

Discuss What You've Read

Name _____

Book Chat Guide

You may want to use the questions below for discussion after reading each group of chapters or after finishing the book.

Chapters 1–4

Chat About Character

A good detective investigates all suspects! What have you learned about each of the characters in the book so far?

Your Own Questions

_____

_____

Chapters 5–8

Chat About Plot

As the play rehearsals continue, what events occur that increase the tension of the actors? Who do you suspect is the culprit?

Your Own Questions

_____

_____

Chapters 9–12

Chat About Plot

Mystery stories have plots that twist and turn. What surprising plot twists confuse the Bean brothers?

Your Own Questions

_____

_____

Chapters 13–16

Chat About Climax

The excitement builds in a mystery story until the mystery is solved. Who solves this mystery? How?

Your Own Questions

_____

_____

Reading Contract

I _____ agree to read *From Anna*.
your signature

After looking through *From Anna*, I will read it to find out:

_____

Write your own purpose for reading here.

_____

I plan to read *From Anna*:	Date you think you'll finish	Date you did finish
☐ straight through		
☐ or in groups of chapters		
Chapters 1–5		
Chapters 6–10		
Chapters 11–15		
Chapters 16–20		
Activities I plan to do:		
☐ Activity Card 14: Respond activity 1, 2, or 3 (Circle your choice.)		
☐ Activity Card 14: Project Time activity 1, 2, or 3 (Circle your choice.)		

✏ S O M E T H I N G   E X T R A

Track Events As you read, make a time line of events for yourself. Then, next to each event, jot down how you would feel if you were Anna.

Name _____

Write About Moving to a New Country

Imagine your family was moving to a new country where people spoke a language you didn't understand. What problems do you think you would have? In what ways would you enjoy moving to a new country? Jot down your thoughts on the chart.

Moving to a New Country

	What I might like about . . .	What I might find difficult about . . .
Learning a new language		
Making friends		
Going to a new school		
Family life		

Name _____

Show What Happens to a Character

When Anna's family moves from Germany to America, Anna's life changes in many ways. As you read, write down the most important thing that happens to Anna in each of the places where she spends time. You can refer to your diagram during your book chat if you wish.

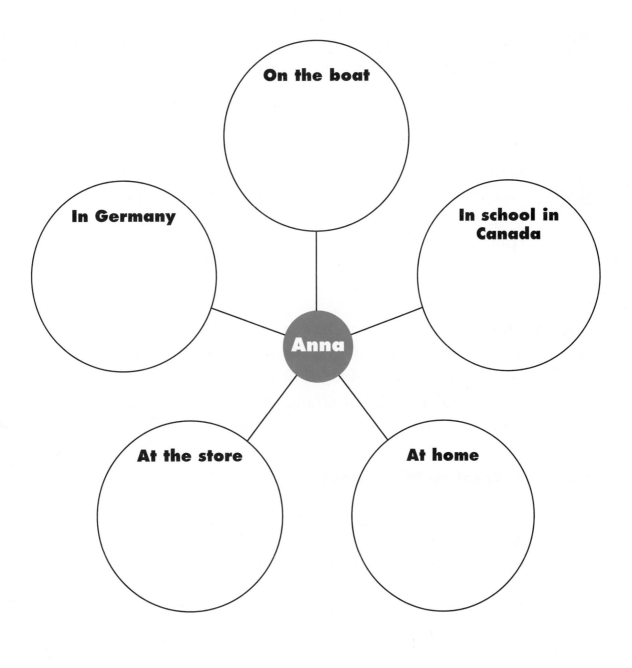

Name _____

Book Chat Guide

You might want to discuss *From Anna* after you've finished the book. You can use the questions below to begin your chat. Write your own questions for discussion as you read.

Chat About Events

Papa promised Anna that she would grow up where thoughts are free. What events showed that Papa might not be able to keep his promise if their family remained in Germany?

Chat About Character

Anna could not read and she was the clumsy one in the Solden family. What caused her to change as the story progressed? How did the response of Anna's family and friends change?

Chat About Mood

The mood of the story changes when the Solden family moves from Germany to Canada. What was the mood while they lived in Germany? What was it as they were traveling to Canada? How did it change when they arrived in Canada? What was the mood by the end of the story?

Things You Want to Talk About

_____

_____

_____

Reading Contract

I _____ agree to read
your signature

The Adventures of Spider: West African Folktales. After skimming *The Adventures of Spider*, I want to read it to find out:

_____

Write your own purpose for reading here.

I plan to read *The Adventures of Spider:*	Date you think you'll finish	actual date you finished
☐ straight through		
☐ by story		
How Spider Got a Thin Waist		
Why Spider Lives in Ceilings		
How Spider Got a Bald Head		
How Spider Helped a Fisherman		
Why Spiders Live in Dark Corners		
How the World Got Wisdom		
Activities I plan to do:		
Activity Card 15: Respond activity 1, 2, or 3 (Circle your choice.)		
Activity Card 15: Project Time activity 1, 2, or 3 (Circle your choice.)		

✎ **S O M E T H I N G   E X T R A**

Journal Idea As you read, you might want to jot down any questions you might have about spiders or other animals you read about.

Before You Read

Name _____

Write Answers to Letters

You are Spider. Make up answers to the questions some children have asked about you.

Dear Spider,
Why do you spin a web in the corner of my room?
Rosa

_____
_____
_____
_____
_____

Dear Spider,
How did you get such a thin waist?
Mike

_____
_____
_____
_____
_____

Dear Spider,
Why do you have eight legs?
Kiyo

_____
_____
_____
_____
_____

Dear Spider,
How can you walk straight up a wall and not fall down?
Andi

_____
_____
_____
_____
_____

Think As You Read

Name _____

Make a Story-Comparison Map

A story-comparison map can help you keep track of the characters, settings, story events, and endings of stories. Use this map to compare two or three of the Spider stories. What similarities and differences can you find? You might want to bring along your story map if you have a book chat with someone else who has also read the Spider stories.

Story A	Story B	Story C

Characters:

Characters:

Characters:

Setting:

Setting:

Setting:

Most important event:

Most important event:

Most important event:

What finally happens?

What finally happens?

What finally happens?

© Scott, Foresman and Company

Discuss What You've Read

Name _____

Book Chat Guide

You might want to discuss *The Adventures of Spider* after you've finished the book. You can use the questions below to begin your chat. Write your own questions for discussion as you read.

Chat About Plot

Talk about what Spider tries to accomplish in your favorite story. How does he try to reach his goal?

Chat About Character

Lazy Spider always seems to try to "get something for nothing." But what happens each time? How do the other characters catch on to Spider's foolishness?

Things You Want to Talk About

_____

_____

_____

_____

Texas Writing Practice

Texas writing masters are linked to both the *BookFestival* trade books and to the TAAS writing objectives. Each master begins with a prompt that asks students to connect selection-specific ideas or events with their personal knowledge and experience. Two pictorial prompts are provided to give students practice writing in response to picture cues.

Writing Master	TAAS Writing Prompt	Selection
1 *	Descriptive Writing: A Letter (Informative/Descriptive)	*The Girl Who Loved the Wind*
2 *	Narrative Writing: A Story (Expressive/Narrative)	*The Mouse and the Motorcycle*
3	Descriptive Writing: A Character Sketch (Informative/Descriptive)	*There's a Boy in the Girl's Bathroom*
4 *	Explanatory Writing: A Letter (Informative/Narrative)	*Night Markets*
5	Narrative Writing: A Story (Expressive/Narrative)	*Sidewalk Story*
6 *	Informative Writing: An Article (Informative/Classificatory)	*Tales of a Fourth Grade Nothing*
7 *	Persuasive Writing: A Letter (Persuasive/Descriptive)	*Staying Nine*
8	Explanatory Writing: An Article (Informative/Narrative)	*Willie Mays, Young Superstar*
9	Informative Writing: A Composition (Informative/Classificatory)	*Esio Trot*
10	Informative Writing: A Letter (Informative/Classificatory)	*Sarah, Plain and Tall*
11	Persuasive Writing: A Letter (Persuasive/Descriptive)	*Grandma Moses, Painter of Rural America*
12	Descriptive Writing: A Composition (Informative/Descriptive)	*Kickle Snifters and Other Fearsome Creatures*
13	Explanatory Writing: A Report (Informative/Narrative)	*The Case of the Sabotaged School Play*
14	Persuasive Writing: A Composition (Persuasive/Descriptive)	*From Anna*
15	Narrative Writing: A Story (Expressive/Narrative)	*The Adventures of Spider*

* = a writing model is provided for this prompt

Using the Writing Prompts

The writing prompts provide students with practice in writing using a variety of purposes, modes, audiences, and forms.

- **Purpose:** Students write to persuade, to inform, or to express thoughts or feelings.

- **Mode:** The prompts ask students to tell a story, to describe, or to classify.

- **Audience:** Each prompt specifies an audience, either formal (such as teacher, principal, or local newspaper) or informal (parent, friend, classmate, and so on).

- **Form:** Students write in a variety of forms, including letters, articles, and compositions.

Using the Writing Models

A sample response for the first occurrence of each type of writing prompt is provided. You might give students copies of the models to keep in their portfolios or make transparencies of the models to use for demonstration. See Writing Masters 16–20.

Assessment

Your students' Texas test compositions will be evaluated according to a system called *focused holistic scoring*. To assess your students' practice compositions according to this system, evaluate how well the paper communicates as a whole. These questions may serve a guide:

- Does the response address the topic using the correct purpose and mode?

- Is the style appropriate for the intended audience?

- Is the information presented in an organized manner?

- Does the student use grade-appropriate spelling and grammar conventions?

Name _____

Descriptive Writing: A Letter

In *The Girl Who Loved the Wind*, the author uses words to paint a picture of the beautiful house and garden Danina's father made for her. Write a letter to a friend in which you describe a beautiful place you have seen. Use details to show what the place is like.

✎ W R I T I N G   T I P S

✔ Before you write, picture the place in your mind and list what you see.

✔ Begin by writing what the whole place is like. Then write about each detail on your list.

✔ Use words that tell where things are located.

Instead of writing: There is a table in the room.
Write: The long, wooden table is in the middle of the room.

Writing
Prompt

Name _____

Narrative Writing: A Story

In *The Mouse and the Motorcycle*, Ralph has exciting adventures with Keith's toy motorcycle. Think of another animal. Write a story for your parents about what happens when you meet this animal. Tell about an adventure the two of you have.

✎ WRITING TIPS

✔ Before you write, plan what will happen in your story. List the events in order, from first to last.
✔ Be sure your story has a beginning, a middle, and an end.

Instead of writing: A pig was eating our food.
Write: I heard a crunch outside the tent. I peeked out. A large pig in bib overalls was enjoying my dinner.

Writing Prompt

Name _____

Descriptive Writing: A Character Sketch

In *There's a Boy in the Girls' Bathroom*, Jeff and Bradley both visit Carla, the school counselor. Carla is memorable in many ways. Think of someone who is memorable to you. Write a description for your parents, telling what this person is like.

✎ W R I T I N G   T I P S

✔ First, jot down what you know about the person. List details about the person's looks and things that make this person special.
✔ Begin your sketch by introducing the person.
✔ Then tell about the person. Use words that tell how he or she looks and acts.

Instead of writing: My brother is funny.
Write: Jess, my red-haired older brother, has a thousand ways to make me laugh.

Name _____

Explanatory Writing: A Letter

Night Markets describes the way people mix, shape, and bake 1,200 dozen rolls for restaurants and stores each night of the week. Write a letter to your friend telling how to make a dish you enjoy eating. Tell what you do first. Then tell about the other steps to take in making the dish.

✎ WRITING TIPS

✔ List the steps you'd take to make the dish in the order that you would do them.
✔ When you write, describe each step separately.
✔ Use words such as *first*, *next*, and *last* to show where one step ends and the next one begins.
✔ Tell your readers everything they'll need to know.

Instead of writing: Heat the milk, but first peel the apples.
Write: First peel the apples. Then heat the milk for two minutes.

Name _____

Narrative Writing: A Story

Lilly Etta wants to help her friend's family in *Sidewalk Story*. Write a story for your best friend in which two friends help each other with a problem in school.

✏ WRITING TIPS

✔ Plan your story before you write. Decide what problem the friends will face, what they'll do about it, and their solution.

✔ Tell where and when events take place. Use words such as *first*, *then*, and *later* to help readers keep track of time.

✔ Be sure your story has a clear beginning, middle, and end.

Instead of writing: The goat ate the paper. Jim tried to stop it.

Write: "No!" cried Jim, jumping to his feet. He was too late. The goat already had the paper in its teeth.

Name _____

Informative Writing: An Article

In *Tales of a Fourth Grade Nothing*, Fudge makes Peter's life interesting—at the very least! Think about what is good and bad about having a little brother or sister. Write an article for your classmates explaining *both* the good and bad points about having a little brother or sister.

✎ WRITING TIPS

✔ Before you write, list good and bad points.
✔ In your article, follow an order that makes sense.
✔ Connect your ideas.

Instead of writing: My brother is annoying. It's good to be admired.

Write: It can be annoying when a younger brother follows you around. On the other hand, it feels good to be admired.

Writing Prompt

Name _____

Persuasive Writing: A Letter

In *Staying Nine*, Rosa Rita convinces Heather that growing older can be fun. If you could choose one age to be for the rest of your life, what age would you choose and why? Write a letter to your grandparents. Tell what age you would choose to be your whole life and give your reasons.

✎ WRITING TIPS

✔ Before you write, list the three best things about the age you've chosen.
✔ In your letter, first tell what age you'd like to be. Then give your reasons.
✔ Write one paragraph for each reason.

Instead of writing: I'd like to be five years old.
Write: I'd like to be five years old forever. When you're five, other people take care of you.

© Scott, Foresman and Company

Writing Prompt

Name _____

Explanatory Writing: An Article

In *Willie Mays, Young Superstar*, Willie's father gives him advice that helps him become an excellent baseball player. Think of an activity that you're good at. Write an article for your school newspaper explaining how to excel at this activity. Write the steps your readers should take, from first to last.

✎ W R I T I N G   T I P S

✔ Before you write, list all the steps you took to learn the activity.
✔ Using your list, explain how to learn the activity. Describe each step separately.
✔ Present the steps in order. Use words such as *first*, *next*, and *last* to keep the order straight.
✔ Make sure your directions are clear and complete.

Instead of writing: Practice roller skating a lot.
Write: First, get a helmet, knee pads, and elbow pads.

© Scott, Foresman and Company

Name _____

Informative Writing: A Composition

Mrs. Silver chooses a tortoise as a pet in *Esio Trot*. There are both good and bad things about keeping tortoise as pets. That, however, is true of almost any animal. Choose one animal that might be kept as a pet. Write a composition for your teacher explaining *both* what would make this animal a good pet and what would make it a bad pet.

✏ W R I T I N G   T I P S

✔ Before you write, list the good and bad points about the pet.
✔ Use words and phrases such as *but* and *on the other hand*.
✔ Use specific examples to show what you mean.

Instead of writing: Cats can cause damage to your house, but they're still good pets.
Write: Cats scratch the furniture. On the other hand, they take care of themselves.

Name _____

Informative Writing: A Letter

In *Sarah, Plain and Tall*, Sarah Elisabeth Wheaton considers both the good and bad points about living on the prairie and decides to stay there. Write a letter to a friend explaining *both* what is good and what is bad about where you live.

✎ W R I T I N G   T I P S

✔ Before you write, list the good and bad points.
✔ Use words such as *both*, *neither*, and *but*.
✔ Be specific! Give examples to show what you mean.

Instead of writing: It's not great in the winter where I live.
Write: Winters are hard in my town. It snows all day, everyday.

Writing Prompt

Name _____

Persuasive Writing: A Letter

Grandma Moses, Painter of Rural America is a biography of an American painter who has won many honors. Who can you think of that deserves a special award? Write a letter about this person to your hometown newspaper and explain why he or she should be honored.

✎ WRITING TIPS

✔ Before you write, list what is special about the person.
✔ Begin your letter by introducing the person.
✔ Back up your opinion with specific examples.
✔ Don't just give facts. Remember that your goal is to persuade.

Instead of writing: Uncle Ralph is brave.
Write: Uncle Ralph rushed through a fire to save Jody Greene.

Writing Prompt

Name _____

Descriptive Writing: A Composition

Kickle Snifters and Other Fearsome Critters introduces us to some very strange creatures. How would you describe the creature shown in this picture? Write a composition for your teacher describing what you see.

✏ **WRITING TIPS**

✔ First list every detail you can see about the creature.
✔ Decide the best order in which to present these details.
✔ Remember that your purpose is to describe, not to tell a story.
✔ Use specific details to describe the creature. Follow the order you have decided upon.

Instead of writing: It's a scary-looking creature.
Write: It's red-eyed and ratlike with hair that looks like wire.

Writing Prompt

Name _____

Explanatory Writing: A Report

In *The Case of the Sabotaged School Play*, Sam and Dave Bean use their detective skills to solve a problem—the mystery surrounding the drama club's new play. What problem have you solved? Write a report for your classmates in which you tell how you solved the problem. Explain what you did first. Then tell about each of the other steps you took to solve the problem.

✏ WRITING TIPS

✔ Before you write, list all the steps you took.
✔ When you write, describe each step clearly and completely.
✔ Tell what you did in the order that you did it.
✔ Use words such as *first*, *afterwards*, and *finally* to help your readers follow the order of events.

Instead of writing: I used another bag so the garbage wouldn't spill.
Write: I knew the wet garbage bag would break. To fix it, first I slid the paper bag into a plastic one.

Writing Prompt

Name _____

Persuasive Writing: A Composition

Anna's father makes a choice to move his family from Germany to Canada in the novel *From Anna*. If you could move anywhere in the world, what place would you choose and why? Write a composition for your best friend in which you describe the place you have chosen. Give reasons that will convince your friend to consider moving to this place too.

✎ WRITING TIPS

✔ Before you write, brainstorm reasons to move to this place.
✔ Name the place you want to discuss. Then write a paragraph about each point on your list.
✔ Don't just give information. Use striking words to paint a clear picture.

Instead of writing: Portland is a city in Oregon.
Write: Portland is in scenic Oregon, right between Mt. Hood and a lovely rocky coast.

Name _____

Narrative Writing: A Story

The Adventures of Spider tells a story about a favorite character from West African folklore. Look at the animal in this picture. Write a story for your parents about one of this animal's adventures.

✎ WRITING TIPS

✔ Plan your story before you start writing. List everything that will happen in the order that it will happen.

✔ Tell your story in an order that is easy to follow. Use words such as *first* and *next* to show when each event happens.

✔ Be sure your story has a beginning, a middle, and an end.

Instead of writing: Alika fell down the hill.
Write: Suddenly, Alika felt the ground give way. She was sliding!

Name _____

Descriptive Writing: A Letter

In *The Girl Who Loved the Wind*, the author uses words to paint a picture of the beautiful house and garden Danina's father made for her. Write a letter to a friend in which you describe a beautiful place you have seen. Use details to show what the place is like.

Dear Mike,

    Short Sands is the most beautiful place I've ever seen. It's a beach in Oregon, on the Pacific Ocean.

    The beach is shaped like a horseshoe and the sand is white. The ocean is in front of you. There are huge rocky cliffs at both ends of the beach. The waves crash against the rocks and make spray. You can feel the mist on your face and smell the salt. Sometimes you can see a rainbow. I'm really lucky that my family gets to go to Short Sands every summer.

          Your friend,

            Seth

✎ WRITING TIPS

✔ Before you write, picture the place in your mind and list what you see.
✔ Begin by writing what the whole place is like. Then write about each detail on your list.
✔ Use words that tell where things are located.

Instead of writing: There is a table in the room.
Write: The long, wooden table is in the middle of the room.

Writing Model

Name _____

Narrative Writing: A Story

In *The Mouse and the Motorcycle*, Ralph has exciting adventures with Keith's toy motorcycle. Think of another animal. Write a story for your parents about what happens when you meet this animal. Tell about an adventure the two of you have.

> Fester was a pig. He lived on Uncle Walter's farm. Unlike most pigs, Fester could talk. However, I was the only one who ever heard him.
>
> One day, Fester wanted to drive the tractor. I tried to stop him, but Fester wouldn't listen. Of course, Fester couldn't drive too well. His hoof kept slipping off the pedal. He almost hit a tree. That's when I grabbed the wheel.
>
> Just then, Uncle Walter came out and saw us. He thought I was driving the tractor the whole time. I got in big trouble. I tried to tell him that it was all Fester's idea but he didn't believe me. Good old Fester kept quiet. I never talked to that pig again!

✏ WRITING TIPS

✔ Before you write, plan what will happen in your story. List the events in order, from first to last.
✔ Be sure your story has a beginning, a middle, and an end.

Instead of writing: A pig was eating our food.
Write: I heard a crunch outside the tent. I peeked out. A large pig in bib overalls was enjoying my dinner.

Writing Model

Name _____

Explanatory Writing: A Letter

Night Markets describes the way people mix, shape, and bake 1,200 dozen rolls for restaurants and stores each night of the week. Write a letter to your friend telling how to make a dish you enjoy eating. Tell what you do first. Then tell about the other steps to take in making the dish.

Dear Darcy,

    Fruit juice Popsicles taste great, and they're easy to make. You'll need three things: an empty ice cube tray, a bunch of toothpicks, and fruit juice.

    Here's how to make the Popsicles. First, set a toothpick in each cup of the tray. Next, pour fruit juice into each cup. Then stick the tray into the freezer and wait. Don't take the tray out too soon, or you might spoil the Popsicles. Once the juice is frozen, pull out a Popsicle by grabbing the toothpick. I hope you like them!

Your Friend,

Kate

✎ WRITING TIPS

✔ List the steps you'd take to make the dish in the order that you would do them.

✔ When you write, describe each step separately.

✔ Use words such as *first*, *next*, and *last* to show where one step ends and the next one begins.

✔ Tell your readers everything they'll need to know.

Instead of writing: Heat the milk, but first peel the apples.
Write: First peel the apples. Then heat the milk for two minutes.

Writing Model

Name _____

Informative Writing: An Article

In *Tales of a Fourth Grade Nothing*, Fudge makes Peter's life interesting—at the very least! Think about what is good and bad about having a little brother or sister. Write an article for your classmates explaining *both* the good and bad points about having a little brother or sister.

> There is both a good side and a bad side to having a little brother or sister. I have a younger sister, so I know.
>
> One good thing is that a younger brother or sister looks up to you. I hear my sister bragging about me sometimes, and it makes me feel great. Also, it's nice to have someone to play with any time you want.
>
> There's a bad side too. Younger brothers and sisters are always messing up your stuff and trying to get into your room. They break things. What's worse, they get away with it because they're cute. That can be annoying! Still, I'm glad I have a little sister.

✎ W R I T I N G   T I P S

✔ Before you write, list good and bad points.
✔ In your article, follow an order that makes sense.
✔ Connect your ideas.

Instead of writing: My brother is annoying. It's good to be admired.
Write: It can be annoying when a younger brother follows you around. On the other hand, it feels good to be admired.

Name _____

Persuasive Writing: A Letter

In *Staying Nine*, Rosa Rita convinces Heather that growing older can be fun. If you could choose one age to be for the rest of your life, what age would you choose and why? Write a letter to your grandparents. Tell what age you would choose to be your whole life and give your reasons.

Dear Grandma and Grandpa,

    I wish I could be six years old again. I think six is the best age to be, for three reasons.

    First of all, you can have a lot of fun. You can walk and talk and play. What more could you want?

    Also, you don't have to take care of yourself. Your parents feed you and buy you clothes. They take you to neat places.

    Most important, you get to go to kindergarten. Kindergarten is a blast. You get to paint pictures and play games all day long.

    I think six years old is the best age to be. What do you two think?

                  Love,
                    Sara

✎ WRITING TIPS

✔ Before you write, list the three best things about the age you've chosen.
✔ In your letters, first tell what age you'd like to be. Then give your reasons.
✔ Write one paragraph for each reason.

Instead of writing: I'd like to be five years old.
Write: I'd like to be five years old forever. When you're five, other people take care of you.